MENTAL POWER

MENTAL POWER

POWER

The power of thought

MANUEL TRIGUERO

First edition: January 2022
Title: MENTAL POWER
Cover image: Ben Kraas
Copyright © 2022 Manuel Triguero
ISBN: 9798796775516

To my mother, my true source of wisdom.

Index

Introduction

The one who uses his mental power is the one who knows how to orient himself through life; the one who knows how to consider the possibilities that life offers him; the one who intensifies his efforts when it is worthwhile, and knows how to listen to his "inner voice" which contains all wisdom, and manages to make an interval to enter into that space where understanding is reached, where difficulties are solved and the best path is divined: the most effective way to reach the goals set.

All this power is hidden within us. With a little concentration on our part, if we move away from the unconscious movement of the mind, we can penetrate further and realize the enormous wealth that we hide.

In fact, there we can find the true source of our happiness, from that place is where everything starts, where we reach the mastery of ourselves and correct our mistakes and all those confusions to which we are often subjected.

If we have enough temperance, we can extend ourselves throughout our consciousness to clarify our ideas, to establish an order on all that exaggerated amount of thoughts that we have daily, which are related to an endless number of contents that appear and at the same time are dissolving.

Some of these elements are more transcendental than others, they ascend or descend, according to the importance we give them. Some are easily extinguished and others remain there, for long periods of time, inviting us to understand life in a certain way.

Your mental power is based on the knowledge of the principles that govern your mind, on knowing how to decipher all those elements that make up your inner world, which are hidden, but which at the same time appear in a resplendent way, capturing all your attention, filling every space of your consciousness and making judgments about you and the world around you.

1. Mental functioning

Our mind is what drives us practically most of the time. Sometimes we make mistakes because we let it choose, it chooses the most convenient decision, and we do not dedicate time to reflection: to foresee the consequences that a given action may bring us.

We often act with urgency, without considering our actions. We only obey the first thing that comes to our mind; that is why the consequences are unpredictable, even if we try to find justifications afterwards.

Your balance depends on what is represented in your mind. If you think too much about a certain subject, it can affect you in such a way that you can become dominated by all those thoughts that pile up to the point of subduing you, causing you to fall into confusion.

Our mind is impulsive and works in a constant way. Sometimes it confuses us with false illusions and expectations, through a series of thoughts that rise from our memory and that are increasing by joining with other similar ones; in such a way that in the end they become a mixture of intentions that incline us to act in a certain way, to develop a series of actions with a concrete course.

We can contemplate how our imagination often determines us, dressing the facts with a false veil that in nothing corresponds to reality.

We can complicate our existence unnecessarily, giving importance to things that do not have it. We can attribute a different meaning to everything that happens to us, so that sometimes we come to deny reality, through conjectures that only exist in our own imagination, without valid, weighty arguments.

It is evident that our mind can also play tricks on us; it can lead us to fall into a terrible depression; put obstacles, impediments in everything that we propose to do; prevent us from intervening when we have some doubts; and it can fill us with falsehood, causing us to have an appearance that does not correspond at all with what we are.

It can make us virtuous, help us achieve excellence; or on the other hand it can numb us, immobilize us, silently muzzle us without us being very conscious of it.

Our transit through life depends on how we use it. If we use it properly, we will come to know the magnitude of all our hidden potential. We will even be able to destroy the restlessness, the anguish, every time they appear, because we have enough tools to do it, in a precise way and every time we need it; depending on how our mental conditions are, so will be our life.

We do not know many of its functions, so it is necessary for us to appreciate each small detail that we observe within that sequence of contents that constantly pass through the screen of our consciousness.

This observance will help us to examine in an adequate way all that confluence of information that is cited in that space, which is combined forming a relation of ideas that are dressing the reality in each moment; they are contents that are threaded together, that we are feeding without knowing it and that in the end make us the person we are.

PROJECTION

Everything that happens inside us, is transferred outside. Our sadness, for example, can be clearly seen in the eyes of others. The same happens with the rest of our moods, with everything that is making us feel bad inside.

What we feel inside can either stimulate us, or it can stifle us and push us away from the world with determination, unless we use our own will not to allow it.

The way we understand the world then carries over into our environment, it can be simplified in what we do on a daily basis and the way we do it.

In a way, we are subject to what happens first within us, we are the consequence, in this sense, of our own thoughts, of our way of encasing our ideas. Our life can be a dawning or a darkening, depending on where we focus our mind in each moment.

If inside we feel that there is instability, it will then move outside and be visible to all those around us. It will spread outside. Everything that happens in our mind has an inertia that makes it grow bigger and bigger, until it manages to come out and ends up revealing itself outside, in our immediate environment. It can be easily appreciated in what we do, in the way we behave and in any behavior we carry out. If there is insecurity inside, there will also be insecurity in our own behaviors, no matter how simple they may be.

The influence of our mind, therefore, does not end inside, it also spreads in all those aspects of our personality that are easily perceived by those around us.

Everything is connected. If our way of thinking is irrational, our way of expressing ourselves to others will also be irrational. If within us there is restlessness and we are not at peace with ourselves, we will also project this outwardly and in the same way this will also be appreciated outside.

Everything we conceive in our mind has a consequence. It can lead us to success or to the most resounding failure. Our way of thinking is projected on the outside. All that spring of images that are represented in our conscience in the end becomes all the behaviors that we manifest on the outside, through the different actions that we carry out.

Therefore, our mind is the one that ultimately leads us. If we recognize what is in it, we will go in the direction that we ourselves decide; if we follow it in an unconscious way, without being attentive to our thoughts, we will allow it to be the one that directs us.

In the latter case our activity will be automatic, we will act like a robot directed by our own mental programming without being very conscious of it.

For these reasons we are obliged to consider, in a more careful way, our thoughts and everything that passes through our consciousness.

We cannot run away from this task, because we can be dragged by all that mental movement that exists within us and that sometimes we are unable to stop because we do not understand very well how it works.

We have to understand that everything that spreads inside us then spreads outside, through what we do every day, through our own behaviors and the way we relate to those around us; everything we feel inside then has a consequence outside of us.

PROGRAMMING

We must deviate from everything that our mind proposes to us at every moment, because not always what arises in our conscience automatically is the best for us.

Surely all these contents obey a previous programming that we have been reinforcing over time, focusing on certain thoughts and giving relevance to some mental contents. In this way we manage to repeat them constantly, occupying practically most of the space in our consciousness, clouding other contents that may be more important to us.

Our mental mechanism is subjected to this programming that we feed day by day, without being very conscious of it.

We remain immobile, without realizing that it is necessary to react in order to change the direction of our own mind, of that which occupies a space in our consciousness that distances us from what we are and distances us from that center where we find ourselves.

In the end, our life becomes everything that we constantly think, in all those occurrences that come to our head and that little by little form a structure that is then expressed in our language, in our own actions; that in many occasions lead us to acts that lack a determined sense, that we only do them to continue with that tendency that starts in our mind, in which there is no order and can become a chaos if we do not master it; if we do not patiently observe its characteristics and perceive them in all their dimension, getting to grasp the direction that many thoughts have, especially those that lead us to move in one direction and that have been previously programmed by ourselves.

SOURCE OF DIFFICULTIES

There is a whole world within you that occupies your inner space, which is like a restless current that feeds your thoughts and makes you keep your attention on some subject, on some matter; sometimes it even forces you to act imperiously, without stopping to examine the consequences. At other times it can limit you, it can take possession of you and paralyze you, distract you along strange and contradictory paths that lead you to suffering.

Everything we do emanates from our mind, everything is sustained by it. Sometimes, a lot of information accumulates there and our reasoning and our internal discourse are adulterated, they appear disordered and our vision of reality changes.

In our mind is created our own restlessness, our indecision, that which saves us or everything that diverts us from the path, that robs us of our freedom and keeps us clinging to our thoughts, without us being able to maintain a certain independence.

When we find ourselves in a situation of hopelessness, of suffering, we must stop and observe our mental system, which is where it all starts. It is there where our frustration is generated; where we become infected with pessimism and simulate a parallel world that in the end has nothing to do with the real one.

When we are victims of anguish or worry, it is also necessary to recognize that everything starts from the same place, from our own mind, which is capable of oppressing us until it enslaves us; or it can protect us from all those strange impulses that agitate us inside and make us move in restlessness, in a constant way.

In our mind can reign fear, restlessness in a permanent way. It can cause us to be hasty, thoughtless and our judgments are not calm; it can cause us to live in a permanent altercation, in a state of shock; it can cause us to live a life without any satisfaction, without any joy.

The mind is a mechanism that is capable of solving many inconveniences, but it can also lead us to melt into sadness, when it diverts us or brings us closer to thoughts that confuse us, in such a way that they take us away from tranquility.

It is in our own mind where we find the impediments that paralyze us, that we remain suspended when we try to take the initiative to try to undertake some project or create something else that is important to us. Everything stems from there, even the way we understand the world and the way we communicate with others.

Some thoughts that rush through your mind, can isolate you, can submerge you in a disinterest in life that can numb you and make you subordinate to them, without hardly having the opportunity to grow inside, to be able to meditate and reflect on the important things that happen to you, on those secrets that are kept deep inside yourself.

If you let yourself be carried away by your mind, by that powerful movement that little by little is growing, determining you, you will lose your balance and you will get involved in actions that in the end will end up being installed as habits that will take possession of you, of your will -as you feed them-.

If you allow your mind to direct you internally, you will notice that every day you have a different purpose, that your aspirations move depending on where the wind blows, and that many of your efforts are not worth it because they are made according to each thought that arises in your mind, which captures your attention until it finally manages to direct you.

What to do

In those moments it becomes necessary that you aspire to more, so as not to be affected by all that volume of thoughts that cling you to some ideas that are accumulating inside you and that end up wearing you out, because you resign yourself to believe in them while your life is getting worse without any kind of stimulus; until you fall into discouragement, as if you were chained, forced to stick to that mechanism that is lodged within you that makes your life rush, that is disintegrates and you move away from what is your true purpose: Which is the one that has to do with your "essence", with what you really are.

We cannot live outside of ourselves, because we will be deceiving ourselves; we will let our mind confuse us with an avalanche of false illusions that chain us, entertaining us, and developing in us a whole series of false hopes that in the end can sink us even more, when we finally prove that they are not valid.

Discovering all this is also part of our true mental power. It will help us to dismantle all that deceptive structure that originates in our own mind and that leads us to confusion.

We cannot allow ourselves to be absorbed by this surprising mechanism that little by little is relentlessly constricting us and taking over our will, preventing us from considering other possibilities.

If you do not interpose yourself, if you do not establish a distance between you and all those impressions that appear in your mind, you will be introduced into a world created only in your brain.

When you want to suppress them, you must be aware of all that is spread in your mind. It is the only way to use all that multitude of images that are established in your consciousness in an arbitrary way.

It is the only way to turn off all that mental confusion that often limits you and distances you from "what you really are"; you will understand that everything arises from a relationship of contents that in the end end guide you.

Only if we know that this mechanism works in this way, we can understand its movements, re-establish normality within us and put an end to the suffering that sometimes imposes itself within us because of this way of functioning.

When all this ceases, we find balance, which is important for us, because thanks to it we naturally experience a favorable peace that gives us the opportunity to deviate from all that mental noise and free ourselves from all that thoughtless confusion, caused by those thoughts that spread in our consciousness coming from our memory.

Everything that destroys you is also within you; the malicious thoughts, that which causes you uneasiness and all those ideas that hit you inside in a quiet way, that guide you towards a vision of things that you hold in time and then abandon unexpectedly, when you realize that it is a mistake to maintain those principles that do not lead you to anything.

We can make all those mental elements fade away; or we can multiply them, depending on how we use the mechanism: our mental power.

We can reflect and improve our vision of things, of reality; or we can follow all those unconscious movements that occur in our mind, entrust everything to our imagination and abandon ourselves to the fate of all those thoughts that congregate in our consciousness and that sometimes arise without any criteria, as loose components that are repeated over and over again without a specific task.

It all depends on the way we use our mind. We can submerge ourselves in a world full of worry, of restlessness; or we can insist on those things that produce wellbeing, that contribute to our own development and that lead us to act with moderation and in a healthy way.

Everything depends on that, on the procedure we use to organize and structure our thoughts within it. If we contemplate it we can discover it; know the importance it has; know how all this process works and make the opportune modifications to get used to think in another way, much more calm and with less alterations.

EXTERNAL INFLUENCE

There are many stimuli that influence us throughout the day, in such a way that they direct our actions when we experience their influence. Sometimes they seem tiny, but they turn us on inside and dominate us in such a way that we remain under their influence, which pushes us in a certain direction; this happens on indefinite occasions and can become permanent if we submit to this influence without worrying about the possible consequences that it can bring us.

These stimuli can divert us from the traced path, which can generate imbalance and great uncertainty, since they unconsciously lead us away from our "true purpose" and make us act in an unreflective way, while we simply obey them; sometimes this whole process occurs instantaneously, without us being very conscious of it.

At other times we have to make a decision very quickly and we hardly have time to analyze the messages that come to our mind. This is why we sometimes rush to choose an answer. We do not have enough time to fully understand the situation.

In those cases we need to investigate a little more to have a clear vision of the facts, of the circumstances and of everything that is hidden behind: all those small details that many times go unnoticed but are important for what is happening.

Therefore, in one way or another, we are subject to everything that happens in the world around us. We arrange our behavior according to the stimuli and influences from the outside.

All those facts that happen in the environment in which we live also influence the activity of our own mind. We try to look for reasons to explain all those situations we are seeing before us. We have the need to explore our past knowledge, our stored information, in order to make sense of what we see.

Consequences

All the circumstances and moments that surround us influence us in such a way that they have consequences on our state of mind and our way of understanding life.

In some way we are conditioned by what happens outside; many of our behaviors are based on that. Therefore, we will always be affected by the events that occur in our environment.

Everything is concentrated in that influence outside, which, if we allow it, determines us in such a way that we end up acting under its dominion, following a path that is already marked beforehand, since in the end all our movements are limited to following the steps that are already dictated from outside.

In the end, our activity is predetermined: we build everything according to the external circumstances, to the signals that come to us from outside; to the state of each situation that exists in the context where we live, where we carry out our behaviors.

All external events, in some way, influence us. Our decisions are also determined by everything that happens in our immediate context.

Our present, in some way, is also influenced by the events that happen around us, even if some of them may seem insignificant.

In this way, our decisions seem to be determined when this influence intervenes between us, leading us to change our interests, to take a break, to interrupt our direction and to change our initiatives.

How to act

We cannot be oblivious to that dimension that exists outside, in the world around us: all those setbacks that we have to deal with in the context where we live and all that set of people around us, who in some way also have a great influence on our thoughts and reflections, on our mental structure, after all.

We should not separate ourselves totally from reality. It is important for us to take into account its manifestations; to understand that what happens outside also extends inside ourselves.

We cannot establish a separation between what happens outside and what happens inside ourselves; everything is united, it is part of a system that makes us walk in a certain direction, under the impulses of our own impulses and the influence of the external stimuli that we observe in that space of the world in which we live.

We must also know how to manage this kind of influences so as not to let ourselves be carried away too much by the current, by what prevails at any given moment in society.

2. Mental power

The power of our mind allows us to generate a new reality that is more flourishing, more secure and less influenced by our past.

You can build a new life if you start from there, from that wisdom that gives you the knowledge of all these processes that spread within you.

Our mental power makes it possible for us to follow a certain direction; to set goals and manage our actions to try to achieve them.

If we use it properly, we can change our own habits; stop to analyze the consequences of what we do, taking into account past experiences.

We can take advantage of this ability to act in a more precise way, more adapted to our "true purpose", without destroying anything of who we really are.

You can train yourself in the use of your mental power, use it as a tool that you can manage to improve your external functioning.

Thanks to our mental power, we can stay awake, without deviating from that center that we all have, where we find clarity -the true understanding- and find that inner voice that advises us and takes us away from all that mental noise that often holds us back when it is very intense.

In this way we are able to anticipate, to anticipate what can happen if we act in a certain way. It gives us the power to prevent many mistakes and failures.

To steer that ship that is our mind, it is convenient to reach a certain degree of tranquility, of "inner calm", that helps us to make comprehensible everything that appears disordered within us.

This is the only way to suppress all those limitations of thought that surface every time some content moves through our consciousness.

Now, this cannot be achieved if there is no continuous practice, because we are configured in such a way that our mind never turns off, it works through a continuous loop of incessant thoughts that are repeated over and over again using the same images.

Through practice we can achieve great results, in terms of control of thoughts, and therefore of our own actions and behaviors, especially those that we want to banish once and for all because we understand that they do not cause us any benefit, that they do not take us anywhere.

YOU REACH UNDERSTANDING

Thanks to your mental power you can understand yourself, separate what happens in your mind from what you really are.

Thanks to our mental power we get a glimpse of what is indispensable to continue surviving. It allows us to analyze every circumstance and provides us with enough information to make a decision when necessary.

It is important that we always have the inclination to rise above all these processes to reach an understanding of ourselves. In this way we will find the adequate explanations to all that manifests itself in our mind through a succession of unconscious manifestations that are maintained in time and that sustain our judgments and most of our own beliefs.

When we appreciate and evaluate what we see, we unwittingly come to understand it. And not only that, we can also manage to transform it, to direct it in some way, within that internal dimension where we are moving at that moment.

To move into this internal space means to reach the mastery of everything that is in it.

YOU ESTABLISH ORDER

You can put some order in your inner world; reach an agreement with yourself to subdue any suffering or discomfort that oppresses you internally; tame everything that causes you uncertainty, moderating your thoughts, rejecting those that are not useful to you or that have no basis.

You will be able to change your focus when necessary and you will always be connected with yourself and away from the bad influence of your own thoughts, from all the contradictions they carry with them, and from all those images that divide you and alter you when you immerse yourself in a non-existent, unreal world created by your own imagination.

Thanks to your mental power you can illuminate your conscience, clarify all those mental loops that sometimes get together inside you, driving you crazy, entangling you in a series of behaviors that in the end do not fit with what you are.

If you get used to this practice, you will find enormous benefits in your life. You will live away from confusion, from everything that extracts your energy without you being aware of it; from all those ideas that make you live in a permanent uncertainty in which sometimes you feel stuck for a long time without being able to find a way out.

Thanks to your mental power you can orient all those thoughts with which you are not happy, that separate you from what you are, that are integrated in your own memory and that sometimes draw in your conscience a false vision of reality, that in the end separate you from the world that surrounds you, because they make you rave, through a concentration of beliefs that differ from the truth.

YOU DISCOVER QUALITIES

If you make an effort to insist on conquering that space inside you, dominated by your mind, you will be able to elevate your best qualities.

Your inner growth will be enlarged, for you will have discovered many of the secrets that are kept within you, which are often hidden because you remain subordinate, submissive to the decisions made by your own mind, when you allow it to select for you the contents you should think about and the actions you have to carry out.

If you are not indifferent and you widen your vision of your inner world a little, you will be able to examine all the richness that you have stored within that vast field that you can only observe if you look at yourself, if you remain attentive to all those elements that are assembled in your consciousness and that then become fixed in your memory without your being able to prevent it.

YOU IMPROVE YOUR DEVELOPMENT

The use of our mental power is basic for our development. It can determine what we will end up being; our actions and behaviors; how our emotions will work, and how we will face the difficulties of life.

It can influence our own personal transformation, if we use it properly. It will help us to decipher all those mental enigmas that are hidden in the deepest part of ourselves, that are undefined and that we must investigate and observe, to get all the fruit possible to our true potential that is there, that is inexhaustible and that we have the obligation to know to give continuity to "what we really are"; to develop ourselves properly, examining objectively everything that happens to us; to draw the best possible conclusions from our own experiences and to understand ourselves without the need to destroy ourselves.

Thanks to it you can modify the structure of the mind, you can improve your personal development if you make use of all that wealth that is in your inner world. It allows you to make great changes in your way of understanding reality.

ALLOWS US TO OBSERVE

It gives us the possibility of stopping and observing everything that is dominating us inside, everything that tries to oppress us or makes us ready to execute a series of automatic habits that once started seem to never end.

Our mental power allows us to perceive that which agitates us inside; towards what type of thoughts we are more inclined to, how they evolve within our consciousness and how they are dilated in time if we pay attention to them.

If you use your mental power, you will get to know the causes behind everything we experience within ourselves. You will be able to take advantage of every detail you observe, no matter how insignificant it may be, and you will discover the greatness that lies within you, in your whole mental system, which you can only know if you remain awake, conscious, alert, without letting yourself be subordinated by the thoughts and impulses that continually impose themselves on your consciousness, often in an imprecise manner; if you insist on this, you will come to the understanding of "what you really are".

If there is no moderation on your part of all that is being constructed in your consciousness, you will not have a lucid vision of the world. You must stop to observe, from temperance, the mental objects that move around trying to produce changes in you. You have to be aware that these can increase if you pay attention to them and can break your inner harmony if they are related to negative thoughts or toxic contents.

If you use the power of your mind properly, you will reach balance, moderation; to perceive the existence of all these processes that are running without you being very aware of them. You will be able to distinguish them, to see how they are elaborated and how they make deep changes in you, in such a way that in the end they manage to stop you, to make you go back in what you should not stop.

If we do not pay attention to this we will live permanently in darkness. If we do not get used to examine our thoughts, we will not discover what is behind everything we do, behind our most habitual behaviors. We will accept that we are like that, just like that. We will forget about ourselves and many actions we will do without thinking about the consequences they may have for us or for those around us.

We will be directed by a series of unconscious mechanisms and by a set of processes that little by little we have been programming without realizing it. We will live resigned to obey whatever our mind dictates, we will comply with it to the letter.

If we really use our mental power, we can establish a channel of communication with ourselves, controlling all these movements and protecting ourselves from all that mental activity that in the end ends up distancing us from who we really are.

If we get used to reflect on what we observe in our inner world, we can interrupt all that incessant stream of images that exists in our mind and that is slowly taking over us.

REDUCING NEGATIVE CONTENT

The information we handle on a daily basis is abundant. Therefore, it is necessary that we reduce, as far as possible, all those insignificant contents, all those aspects that limit us, that extinguish our light. Only in this way can we put an end to everything that pushes us to suffering, that is constantly hitting us and consuming us from within.

In a certain way, your well-being also depends on this, on reducing as much as possible all those mental ideas full of difficulty, which sometimes appear in your mind without your permission, inciting you to stop acting in a certain way.

We must be careful of everything that appears in our mind, there are many elements that take over our initiative, that alter us and that dominate us, occupying practically all our attention, while we are content to follow, without regard, those impulses that resist to disappear along our own consciousness.

We can use our mental power to get out of the darkness, to stop all that transference of contents that stun us and to which we get used to and do not stop to recognize; to examine to see if they can produce some kind of disorder.

If you use the power of your mind you will be able to overcome all those representations that sometimes become a deception that dominates you and that you have to obey, and from which you cannot free yourself so easily.

If you use your mental power you will be able to still all those negative contents that expand within you; all that which causes you confusion, which is associated with affliction and restlessness.

You will be able to suppress everything that leads us to our own destruction: all those negative ideas about the world and about ourselves that manifest in our mind, that are scattered throughout our consciousness, and that limit us and establish a somewhat mistaken vision of things.

Thanks to our mental power we can manage to stop all that impetuous force that some thoughts have, when they settle in our consciousness without hiding. We can prevent them from rising, from escalating, from acquiring importance, from becoming frequent and absorbing us completely. We can mitigate them, prevent them from accumulating and joining with each other, from drowning us when they try to confuse us and separate us from reality.

There is the possibility of being able to get rid of them. We only have to be aware of them, to know what they are, to know what it is that holds us back, no matter how insignificant it may seem; what it is that sows us with doubts, that takes away our peace, that agitates us from within, plunging us into an abyss of misfortune and obstacles.

3. The power of thought

If we observe our marvelous inner world, we will realize that it is a constant explosion of thoughts in the form of images that sometimes pass by indifferently, without us valuing them too much; and at other times they lead us to exhaustion, because they overtake us when they are repeated impulsively.

There are innumerable thoughts that we have daily. Sometimes they manipulate us, we allow ourselves to be manipulated by them; others are harmful to our mental health, as they do not benefit us in any way: they dirty our conscience with eccentric artifices that are linked to each other while we feed them without realizing it.

Our way of thinking can limit us and prevent us from progressing. In these cases, we will be misusing our intelligence. If we get used to the fact that the same contents are always being reproduced in our mind, we can let ourselves be trapped by obsession, by a way of thinking that will always be the same.

If this leads to conflict, we will live in permanent confusion; we will act without a solid foundation and we will not be able to understand reality.

If everything that manifests itself within us does not correspond to the truth, and drags us into restlessness and lack of coherence, it will lead us to frustration and failure.

Our thoughts extend further, they are transformed into actions; somehow there is rivalry between them. Many of them try to lead us to a certain behavior, but the one that finds the right content at the right time is the one that finally transforms into action.

In many occasions our answers to the same fact are contrary, depending on the moment in which we are; this is because we do not examine ourselves in a serene way and we let ourselves be carried away by this mental movement of thoughts that upset us, that surround us, moving us away from our true center, from what we really want to be.

If there is no understanding on our part, no order in our ideas, we will persist in doing things in an unconscious way, in acting without taking into account the consequences, following the tendency of our own thoughts, as they arise in our mind. They will be the ones that decide what we are at each moment.

Everything that is reproduced in our mind remains imprinted in our memory, and everything that abounds in our memory then comes to the light of consciousness, in one form or another.

In this way we can see how thoughts evolve, how they emanate from the depths of our memory, which drives them until they are organized throughout our consciousness, and after a short time they disintegrate, giving way to new ones, in an endless stream of contents that does not stop and that little by little constitutes the foundations of what we do every day; it manages our behaviors, our ways of thinking, our beliefs.

In this way, thoughts take hold within us, without a concrete direction, in an anarchic way, reproducing themselves over and over again, forcing us to take a concrete direction, as long as we allow it.

Although we have the capacity to decide, to put a limit to all that maelstrom of thoughts that often impress us. We can move our attention wherever we want, leave aside the imagination and all those unreal contents that often take over us.

We only have to be indifferent and observe everything from tranquility, without letting ourselves be dominated by the force of our mind;

by the vividness of all those thoughts that suddenly besiege us, fomenting in us restlessness.

REPETITIVE THOUGHTS

Not everything we think is really useful. Many repetitive thoughts come to our mind that lead us nowhere.

They involve an expenditure of energy that we cannot recover and a great waste of time, because they make us maintain our focus of attention in a series of contents that in principle are not necessary to us, nor are they related to what is really important to us.

In those moments we must know how to detect them in time, to remove them from our mind and not to stop even for a moment on them.

For this we have to exercise ourselves in trying to govern, as far as possible, all those automatic thoughts that appear in our mind and that captivate us in such a fascinating way that they lead us to a fictitious dream, that makes us forget everything that is happening; that causes us not to be awake and that deceives us by diverting our attention only towards those things that in the end end end up producing pain and suffering, and an anguish that torments us little by little through a series of thoughts that are having a place in our own conscience.

We can clearly observe our authentic mental power when all those impulsive and impetuous contents begin to diminish, when we begin to install within us a silence that occupies all that space in our consciousness that is becoming hollow, as the thoughts that frequently occupy it diminish; then you begin to see that everything becomes clearer, that everything seems simpler and easier and you begin to calm down; while your mind quiets down and the pain and suffering no longer infuriate you so much, since everything begins to melt in that state of stillness, away from the confusion that many times is slowly bringing you down.

This is only possible if you distance yourself from what you apparently observe and do not allow yourself to be confused by the exaltation of all those repetitive thoughts that are mixed, combining within the space of your own consciousness, through a permanent turmoil that separates you from that stillness where you always find temperance.

In this way we will learn to give more relevance to those mental elements that really matter to us: which are those that have to do with what we must really do to feel that we are ourselves, in each moment; to feel fulfilled; to act in accordance with our "true purpose".

INTERNAL DIALOGUE

In our internal chatter we are accustomed to give importance to a series of reflections and issues that manifest themselves in our mind and we end up paying attention to them, even if they are not very useful or we do not know very well the purpose that justifies our waste of time on those issues.

We simply limit ourselves to repeat over and over again within our internal dialogue the same ideas and thoughts, which never seem to end.

We compile from our memory a series of contents and we get hooked to them in such a way that we only see in our conscience the same elements; and with them we carry out a dialogue with ourselves with which we identify ourselves and try to understand what we are living in those moments.

It is a way of communicating with our inner world. When we talk to ourselves, we make visible all those thoughts that are agglomerating in our mind, putting our attention on them, appropriating those that most agree with the situation in which we find ourselves at that moment. If it is a daze, we try to look for similar thoughts, to gather them, to put them together to make us understand better that situation and in some way also to confirm our state of mind.

All the judgments we make at that moment will seek to be based on those same thoughts. We have no need to look for different ones, since we have already become accustomed to them from so many times we have reflected on them.

In the end, our way of understanding the world will be shaped by them, it will depend on the permanence of those thoughts in our mind. If it is very long, our idea of life will be related to the meaning of those same thoughts, simply because they are the ones that have persisted the longest in our conscience, because we have approved them without further ado and because of the comfort of not having the obligation to look for new ones; other new deductions; other new reasonings....

We get used to always draw the same conclusions in the face of the same circumstances, to give continuity to the same thoughts, to the same ideas. We limit ourselves to follow the current of the most repeated thoughts, of those that are more frequent, in such a way that we trust them and continue to feed them, even if they do not suit us.

When we talk to ourselves, we always try to be in agreement with what we are thinking at that moment. In reality, it is a way to protect ourselves, to reciprocate, to seek strength, while we pronounce ourselves on a particular issue that at that moment concerns us.

In our internal dialogue we look at ourselves renouncing to any influence from the outside, trying to concentrate on our own thoughts to look for affirmations, explanations of what is happening to us at that moment.

Calming the mind

When you want to pacify your mind and everything that oppresses you inside, you have to establish a communication with your own inner self, observe where there is any setback, any discord, what thoughts are the ones that are persisting in those moments.

You only have to look at your inner dialogue, everything is transferred there, in what you say to yourself when you are not accompanied by anyone.

Surely you will find some wrong reasoning to which you have become accustomed, without realizing that they are altering, that they are provoking in you, by linking with each other, an annoying imbalance that affects your judgments and your way of understanding the world and everything that happens to you in your day to day.

When you feel that you have doubts or that you are distorting reality with a series of reflections that are closer to nonsense than to reason, pay attention to your inner chatter; you will become aware of the thoughts that are trying to dominate you in those moments, of the logic you are using: whether it is leading you to confusion or helping you to clarify things.

If there is an internal disorder, you will be able to get rid of it if it is really hindering you. You can transform those thoughts that are toxic into messages that are more positive for you.

You will soon realize whether or not there is any inconsistency in the way you see reality. Many problems are caused by our own contradictions; or by coming to false conclusions from some of the experiences we have.

If we are lucid enough, if we pay attention to our internal dialogue, we will appreciate in more detail our way of reasoning; it is what sometimes produces this inner division.

Do not let yourself be dominated

You can suppress what oppresses you in a simple way, you only have to interrupt the mental chatter; you must stop to examine it in stillness; then the thoughts will begin to diminish in a sensible way.

Once you know this mechanism you can impose a certain control over all those contents that appear in your mind, you can even articulate other kinds of thoughts very different from those that end up appearing in your consciousness, fruit of that unconscious process in which different contents are united in an automatic way, without you having too much control over them.

It is not a question of forcing anything, it is enough to be conscious, without intervening too much, and to observe how your thoughts are being shaped and oriented towards a certain subject.

Once you pay attention to this aspect, you understand the logic of your mind, and somehow you do not let yourself be dominated by what you are observing; it ceases to be unknown to you.

Thanks to your persistent attention, the power of your thoughts is diminishing and you begin to not feel so infected by their force and energy; somehow you feel separated, you do not let yourself be imprisoned by them, so in the end you do not end up following them in an obedient way, as you usually do.

This would be a great way to modify your way of thinking, just by going to the origin where this process begins you can establish a new direction, new judgments and another evaluation of reality very different from the one you normally do.

4. The power of observation

There is a whole world to discover within you that you can know just by looking inside yourself and intensely observing all that space you occupy; where you will also find that other dimension where there are no thoughts, where all those images that arise in your consciousness and flow like a river without you having chosen them to appear there, cease to exist.

Within us is hidden all that we need when trying to achieve our accomplishments. We should look at ourselves, at our own inner self, for therein lies all the information available.

Our mental power lies in observing everything that manifests itself and that previously remained hidden; in seeing how it is prolonged in time in our mind at the same time that it provokes a series of emotions that distress us or make us happy.

When you use your mental power is when you observe that which agitates you inside; that set of ideas that are the result of a series of thoughts that modify your way of reasoning, your way of understanding the world. If we are complacent with them, in the end, they will ascend even more to our conscience and they will thread with each other, leading us to a fictitious and superficial life.

If we pay special attention to all that expands within us; if we inquire more frequently into our amazing inner world, we will not live subject to the dictates of our own mind.

We will observe in more detail what is going on inside, what is influencing us the most in those moments, and how we can suppress all those ideas that limit us, that agitate us and make us live in constant uncertainty.

OBSERVING TO BE CONSCIOUS

Observing the thought can be very useful to be aware at all times of the mental content and the influence it can exert on us when directing us towards a particular action.

However, we must take into account that, if we do not know how to control this situation very well, all those thoughts that we observe, being very repetitive, can lead us to divert our focus and end up doing an action related to those thoughts.

The idea of observing what happens in our

mind, must be directly related to the fact of being aware of what happens inside ourselves; in no way can it be used to put our focus of attention always on the same thoughts, or to feed somehow those mental loops of which we are victims in many occasions and that take over us without us being very aware of them.

The idea of observing ourselves, should have as its main purpose the discovery of what happens inside our own mind, in order to know the processes that lead us to act in a certain way.

Because in reality we end up becoming what we repeat continuously, so it can be quite useful to know first hand that mental mechanism through which a series of thoughts arise repeatedly until we end up transforming them into a concrete action; which we also maintain over time, giving rise to a series of habits that condition and direct us without us being very aware of them, on many occasions.

This would be the main objective that we should set ourselves when we try to be conscious, to observe that which is produced within ourselves; because if we know how to use this method properly we can put a stop to all that maelstrom of ideas and mental contents that overwhelm us and that form the basis of what we do repeatedly.

When misfortune hits us with force and in

our consciousness only continuous thoughts manifest and remain, which provide us with disorder and contaminate us with a feeling of displeasure, we have to make an effort to explore that space a little more and observe each fragment that arises in our mind.

In this way, we will have an idea of the kind of contents that are unfolding in it; what kind of elements are occupying it.

To access that space and stop all those contents, it is convenient that you project your attention on everything that moves in your consciousness and do not ignore it. If there is no balance there, it is difficult for there to be balance in what you are doing at that moment, because everything is connected; everything is built first in your mind. It is there where the first fermentation takes place; and then it expands, it is distributed in your behaviors and actions.

Everything derives from what is reproduced in your consciousness: the most outstanding things you can do and also all your mistakes, which are the fruit of thoughtlessness and lack of good sense, most of the time.

Only if we do this exercise, we can restore order, eliminate those fractions and anticipate all those elements that try to weaken us.

Don't let yourself be influenced

If you let yourself be confused by your own thoughts, they will end up accumulating and will use up all your energy. They will be the ones that drive your activity and will not diminish; on the contrary, they will settle in your consciousness and will group and connect with other related thoughts, and they will grow over time until you end up getting used to them.

When that happens, you end up internalizing them in the deepest part of yourself; in such a way that when you want to eliminate them it is no longer possible, you no longer have that capacity, because they cling and hide in such a way in your memory that they are never separated from it.

If they remain on the surface there is no problem, but if they go beyond, they settle in the deepest part of yourself, and nothing can keep them away from there.

You can only realize that they exist if you illuminate your mind through a conscious observation, it is the only way to appease all those hidden contents that are kept there forever, submerged in the memory.

When we fall into despondency and a dangerous confusion lodges within us, which robs us of our will and our vivacity, we must increase our attention on those thoughts that try to capture us, in order to be able to somehow push them aside and organize in another way the contents that in those moments are constituting the structure of our mind.

In no way we can let ourselves be abandoned, absorbed by all those signs that invade our mind, that come to impress us in such a way that they monopolize our attention and even our own will.

If we do not allow ourselves to be captivated by these magnetic thoughts, which in some way determine us, it is possible that we do not end up disoriented, that we take over the power of our own mind, re-establishing the necessary order to achieve our well-being.

Only by making a series of modifications and learning to observe while remaining conscious, we can be above the influence that certain thoughts exert on us; we will reach a deeper discovery of many contents that are hidden inside us, but to which we do not usually have access because we usually keep ourselves on the surface.

With a little willpower we can appease their force. We can dissipate, through conscious and reflective observation, those thoughts that produce a disturbance within us and that try to perpetuate themselves. They must meet with oppo-

sition on our part so that in the end they are reduced and do not become obstacles that upset
us even more, that separate us from who we are
and what we should really be doing.

RESTORING BALANCE

We use multiple evasions, trying to keep ourselves busy, and many times we fall into
thoughtlessness, we do not give ourselves that
pause to know if we are conditioned by our own
thoughts.

We need to discover why there is always this
inner struggle within us that invites us to extend
certain thoughts over time; why the same themes
always abound in our consciousness; what is the
origin and the consequences that this entails.

To observe all this can be fascinating, to enter
the majesty of your mind observing the thoughts
that lead you to your unhappiness and those that
lead you to happiness; we can realize what is
harmful, what does not benefit us.

If we remain more time observing ourselves,
we can realize perfectly how this mechanism
works that separates us from ourselves and that
is based on the constant repetition of thoughts;
that in principle do not maintain a constant line,
they simply obey an automated process that
evokes them at its free will, without an establis-

hed criterion.

If you use your mental power you can re-establish the balance that should be in your mind.

Thanks to contemplation we can look, pay special attention to our thoughts, our judgments and everything that is hidden within us, that leads us to confusion and that somehow molds us, since all these contents are then embodied in actions and behaviors that we put into practice in our daily lives.

We should pay more attention to all those phenomena that occur within us, which in reality are the cause of our destiny.

OBSERVING TO GO TO THE ORIGIN

If we go into our inner world, we can anticipate and evaluate many thoughts that we have habitually. In this way we can go to the beginning, where our reasoning and our way of seeing life and ourselves begin.

We can examine, from calmness, the contents of those thoughts if we know how to go deep into them. It is easy to do so because they are diffused and projected in our consciousness, in such a way that they offer us the possibility to observe them and to realize if they are favorable or not for us.

Our mental power gives us the possibility to go to the beginning, to anticipate everything that tries to determine us; to stop everything that imprisons us, that tries to dominate us through a repetitive activity that happens in the very center of our own consciousness.

Everything that arises in our mind is important, nothing is insignificant. Our greatest wealth lies in having the possibility of observing it, and also of letting it pass, once it is reproduced, if we find some benefit in it.

In any case, we can consider whether or not to adhere to everything that appears insistently in our mind; if it is not very useful, it is always advisable to let it pass.

The wise thing to do is to always follow the current of that which makes us strong, which serves to build us up. It is the best way to clean that place, so that irrational judgments and all those kinds of toxic thoughts that slowly spread, covering everything with a deception without any logic whatsoever, do not flourish.

If we do not abandon ourselves and we are aware of all this that is hidden in our mind, we can avoid its influence, to the extent that we identify its trajectory and its own movements.

When anguish predominates in you and the painful memories of the past are not extinguished, examine the motives; observe the origin, when those thoughts begin to sprout that engender in you that restlessness that you cannot purge.

The formula to find out everything that we have kept deep inside ourselves is to observe it.

It is the only way not to get lost in that vicious circle -which most of the times is produced in our mind- of elements that repeat themselves over and over again without any limitation.

It is the best way to be able to govern our own inner world, to order all that mental structure that we have been creating and strengthening over time.

It can be a way to renew ourselves, to get away from all those toxic thoughts that limit us without valuing very well the consequences that it has for us to get used to those contents so foreign to what we really are, deep inside ourselves.

OBSERVING IN ORDER TO KNOW OURSELVES

We will only reach this other level of functioning, in the first place, if we observe ourselves. If we really get to know ourselves, we will discover all those mechanisms that exist within us and that, without being aware of them, condition us and lead us to behave in an unconscious and repetitive way.

And the fact is that we often live being slaves of our own mind, because we lack sufficient knowledge, because we are not observers of ourselves and we are not aware of all that happens in our own interior, in our inner world; because we have our eyes set more outside than inside.

All these conclusions and many others can be drawn from that observation that we should make frequently, in those moments of reflection and meditation, which are good tools to know ourselves better and all that inner workings that often prevent us from being what we should be; to behave as we would like, to feel good about ourselves and find a coherence with "what we really are".

Our mind can be a torment if we allow ourselves to be trapped by it. Only if we manage to glimpse what is hidden, we will be able to accumulate wisdom about its functioning by which we will be able to guess how to improve.

If we manage to gather and properly associate all that information that is presented to us in a disorderly way, we will be able to experience all that power that is within us, which apparently we do not see because we do not exercise it, because we do not make an effort to go beyond what we experience internally.

Only if we go deeper through a proper internal observation, we can develop all those hidden qualities that are housed within us waiting to be discovered.

OTHER BENEFITS

Observation of thought is beneficial if it is done with a certain control and awareness of all that is going on inside ourselves.

Only those who have enough practice in this kind of exercises can lengthen this situation of observation of their own thoughts, to such an extent that all those contents that emerge so often, so repeatedly, are gradually appeased until they find an "inner calm" in which they feel that their mind is clearing of all that mental noise composed of all that series of monotonous and incessant thoughts that arise repeatedly; In such a way that they manage to achieve that no thought catches them and leads them to a determined action, because they manage to become neutral observers, on the margin of all that mental activity that they observe, because they do it maintaining a distance on all that kind of mental contents.

Reaching this point gives them a new vision of themselves, they no longer see themselves as beings dependent on what they think, as beings dependent on their own mind, because they manage to transcend it, to observe it from a higher level.

To that extent, everything that happens at a mental level no longer affects them, since they maintain a separation between their own thoughts and themselves.

From this position they are able to make the best decisions, in the cases in which it is required, since there is a time and a pause that help to select the best options, since the ideas are not crowded.

There is a greater distance between thoughts and this favors and makes possible a more detailed observation of one's own mental contents, which allows to discern, to separate what you consider more useful from what is not; what you consider more beneficial from what is more harmful for you.

All this occurs within that space of observation within your own consciousness, in which one thought after another follows another.

This kind of exercises, in the same way, help us not to act impulsively; not to identify ourselves with the first thing that comes to our mind; not to let ourselves be dragged by all those repetitive thoughts that sometimes come loaded with so much energy that they end up leading you to a series of unwanted actions, which when repeated end up becoming habits that are very difficult to get rid of.

He who manages to take control of this process, can perfectly master himself, what he thinks, what he does.

This requires concentration, a lot of practice and the habitual use of moments of meditation, of inner observation, in which we connect frequently with ourselves and with everything that happens in our own mind.

If we manage to establish a distance between that which is produced in our mind and ourselves, we will place ourselves in a position of observers of that process; in such a way that we will not be so influenced by this way of proceeding that we have at a mental level.

If we achieve this, through practice, we will obtain a great teaching that will serve us for life in general; since our behaviors and our actions, and our way of being in the world and of expressing ourselves will change, it will be very different: we will not be guided by the first thing we think, but everything we do will be the product of what we believe is best for us, in each moment.

Everything will arise from a pause, from a previous reflection, in which we will put aside all those elements that do not serve us, that we consider that are harmful to us; and in this way our actions will be more congruent, they will be more in consonance with what we really are, in the depths of ourselves.

Through observation we can disarm all this mechanism, realize the mental contents that repeat themselves the most; those that torment us or that lead us to a fickle restlessness.

5. The power of knowledge

Your true mental power lies in knowing how your own mind works; in becoming familiar with all its expressions and discovering some of its secrets, which will lead you to lucidity and to find all those explanations that you have always needed to find a sense to all those mysteries that come with some events that happen to us, that we do not know how to interpret because many times they surpass us; in such a way that we do not find the way to delve further to look for a convincing explanation that solves our doubts.

Everything that dwells in our mind can be examined, the transcendent and the simple, everything can be subject to an analysis on our part; everything that moves through our mental space, both that which we already know and that which we cannot qualify.

That is why we can detect everything that agitates us inside, everything that gets in the way, that blocks us or takes us in another undesired direction; all of this we can transform, if we take care of it.

Once we are aware of all that mental activity, we can differentiate what is profitable from what is not; we have the ability to divert those thoughts that mistreat us and bring us closer to personal destruction.

If we are knowledgeable about our own mind, we can use all its power, explore its workings and unveil its best kept secrets. Everything depends on our ability to contemplate its activity, its mechanical way of acting, which endlessly reproduces an endless train of images that are stored in memory.

All this is possible if we dive deep within ourselves, without letting ourselves be confused by all that accumulation of contents that captivate us without us being very conscious of it.

Thanks to your mental power you can look for the foundation: the way in which your ideas, your beliefs and even your own obsessions are formed, some of them irrational, that little by little are stored in you if you do not destroy them in time.

You can perceive how your mind proceeds, reorganizing all the information that comes from outside and managing it according to the interests you have at any given moment.

All this information is invaluable to you, because it serves to provide you with knowledge that can help you to renew yourself; to restore what is necessary; to find the main strengths and straighten the course if your progress is stopped by some setback or setback.

It is continually laid out before us, though not everyone can see it. This requires careful observation of all the flow of content, all those mental fragments that circulate through our consciousness and the position they occupy; whether they diminish or strengthen; whether we consider them important or not.

It may be an unknown world to us, but if we introduce ourselves into it and take an interest in its functioning, in the end we will obtain the faculty to understand it and to take advantage of all its possibilities.

It all depends on the importance we give to all that moves within our inner world, which often takes possession of us for no apparent reason and separates us from reality.

He who uses his mental power, knows at all times what is most convenient, what is most important. He has an awakened mind, which always finds the best way to proceed; it is only necessary to penetrate a little at an internal level to catch all this knowledge.

KNOWLEDGE OF ONESELF

It is convenient to reflect from time to time on the meaning of your life; on the type of person you are becoming. Whether or not you are far away from "what you really are".

It is about taking advantage of the knowledge accumulated through experience to observe your development; to see clearly if there is order in your life, or if on the contrary it is all a compendium of difficulties created by yourself over the years.

It is advisable to take some time to look into all those secrets that are kept inside you. It is the best way to extract the best of ourselves; to overcome ourselves; to go a little deeper into what we really are.

It is becoming more and more necessary to reach that encounter with oneself to know how to appreciate everything that extends in our inner world; in that space where we find a deep liberation, because we forget everything that oppresses us and all those false contents that adulterate reality and run over our reason.

That is why we must begin to regulate all that mental mechanism, which on many occasions separates us from what, deep inside ourselves, we really want to be; so there must be that connection, that union with that other part of our consciousness, where tranquility reigns, which is purified because in it there is no movement, no activity that leads us in a particular direction.

Becoming what we really are

Not everything that is shown in our mind is what we are; many of these contents are nothing more than mere movements that extend without order throughout our consciousness. From time to time we see them, spontaneously, and we allow ourselves to be deceived into believing that those elements we observe have to do with our own identity.

If we live distant from ourselves and everything that happens inside us, we will never understand what we do or who we are.

It is important that we inspect further, to find out why we identify ourselves with certain thoughts, with some concrete ideas and not with others; why the same contents almost always flourish in our consciousness and why the same images are frequently repeated, which almost always point us in the same direction.

It is good for us to know at all times why we always end up doing the same behaviors, why we have configured ourselves in a particular way, through the repetition of the same behaviors.

If we get used to stop and see the influence that has all that is produced within us, we will find the meaning to many questions that many times we have asked ourselves throughout our lives, about some important issues.

We will discover the origin of what we are and why we walk in the direction we do; we will find ourselves, among all that complexity of information accumulated over time.

Thanks to all this knowledge, we will reach an inner balance that will give us back peace and "inner calm", and "clarity" and understanding of ourselves; our interest in knowing ourselves more will increase and will never die out.

We will recognize the importance of everything that moves in our mind; how it influences us to follow certain thoughts; and how we define ourselves with every action we take, which in the end becomes a faithful reflection of the mental activity that takes place inside, in that incombustible and productive internal space that many times does not allow itself to be governed.

It becomes necessary, therefore, that we use all the power of our mind to become what we really are, so that we become masters of our own destiny and become increasingly aware of everything we do, of everything we think; so that everything has an order and a sense that lead us to our own transformation at the time we need it.

He who discovers his mental power knows his true purpose and does not deviate from it, even though misfortunes may break him and he may go astray along the way.

INNER WORLD

Within us there are many secrets to be discovered, which are surely unused because of the lack of knowledge we have about them.

We must try to probe within ourselves, penetrating a little beyond what we usually see in our own consciousness, to realize the breadth of our inner world, all that space that remains away from the confusion and traps of the mind.

We can only access it if we seek a moment of tranquility, when we manage to silence all that mental noise, all that extensive movement, which always exists within ourselves, of representations that arise again and again, that have no beginning and no end.

Then we will establish a much deeper communication with ourselves; more unalterable, where we can limit ourselves only to observe - beyond the din of our own thoughts- all that harmonic firmament that is our consciousness without content, without forms.

In this way, we will reach a stillness without opposition, an unusual silence, which will invade us completely, which will lead us to know that other unknown part of ourselves; that other part that has to do more with our own being and that some call "Presence"; when we are really present, we are enveloped in that calm that ascends throughout our body, ordering everything in a surprising way.

In this way we can order our inner world a little and incorporate those elements that help us to achieve our goals.

It is a matter of directing our attention to concentrate only on our best resources, always trying to get the best out of ourselves and to improve every day by exercising our best qualities, which we can only develop if we discover where they are housed.

Empty space

We only need to look a little deeper, to go into that seemingly empty space beyond our own thoughts, to realize all the wisdom that is stored there.

At first it may seem that there is nothing, but then time stops, calm begins to reign and you feel free of any bondage.

You begin to appreciate a peace that dwarfs the activity of thoughts, you feel lighter and you do not remember the past or let yourself be contaminated by any idea, or by those false beliefs that often haunt your mind.

It is a secret, mysterious place, usually ignored by most. It is a space that goes unnoticed because most of the time we are disconnected from it, because we are more interested in attending to everything that our mind dictates to us at any given moment.

Only those who have the ability to focus on that space where there are no thoughts will understand it. Only they will be able to obtain the benefit of the "inner calm": that peace that can only be felt there, in that unusual and at the same time fruitful place where you can experience an encounter with yourself, where you learn to know yourself and who you really are.

Only people with a certain degree of curiosity and observation can access this other, somewhat deeper dimension that lies within you.

What is not manifested

We must launch ourselves into the search for our own secrets, which do not manifest or flourish in our consciousness, for they lie beyond: where our "essence", what we are, is glimpsed.

It is a place that is not defined by thoughts, which can only be accessed through tranquility and silence, through an inner calm that diminishes mental activity, that makes us probe, scrutinize in that vast space that is our consciousness without thought, without images.

We can only access it from a contemplative attitude, through which we can observe, establishing the corresponding pause, a constant harmony, which spreads, transforming our inner world into a vast place where everything becomes clear; where you acquire true knowledge and imagination no longer dazzles you, leading you to deception.

It is like a fertile ground for you to fertilize with the thoughts that seem most opportune to you; it is as if your normal mental state were to fade away and in its place a new, more harmonious consciousness, less superficial and closer to what you really are, is propelled.

Your true mental power lies in realizing it, in seeing clearly that which is not frequently manifested in your mind: that which lies beyond, in an inactive way, which is not expressed, but is transcendental, for there is stored what you are. In that room your creativity is also housed, although apparently you only find an emptiness.

To transcend all that movement that occurs in our mind, in which sometimes thoughts arise that do not correspond to the truth of things, it is necessary to go a step further, to go to a higher level of consciousness from which we can observe all this that happens in our mind from another position, as a spectator outside all those thoughts.

Then you will understand that your mental power is also there, in all these possibilities offered by this capacity of conscious observation of all that space that lies beyond your own unconscious thoughts; at that level of consciousness where initially there is only emptiness and silence.

Limiting ourselves to observe

Sometimes we do not go deep enough to reach that point where we find the absence of thoughts and our mind calms down, and everything becomes an emptiness full of silence in which we are immersed, far from suffering and any other influence.

In those moments it is as if we merge with ourselves, as if everything flows in a different way; we do not feel the need to identify ourselves with everything that passes through our mind, as we normally do.

In such a state the affliction ceases to arise and we begin to experience a sense of happiness that was hidden there, but that until that moment we did not have the capacity to feel; it is as if we were observing everything from another approach closer to the truth.

In that situation we limit ourselves to listen and observe everything that we experience within ourselves; we can only reach such a position out of curiosity to know everything that is at a deeper level, which is only in that center where true knowledge exists; where any confusion disappears; where we move away from anguish and any suffering, which is only ignited by all those thoughts that sprout again and again from our mind, in an unconscious and repetitive way.

Our mind is a trap that can wear us out. When we go through bad times, we have to place ourselves in that space where our thoughts are being geared, to try to direct them in some way.

In fact, our mental power is based on that, in being able to push away all those useless contents that are rising in our mind trying to put us on track, to direct us towards a direction that may not suit us too much.

Thanks to meditation we can observe that light that exists within us, which leads us to know how we really are, beyond the external world.

Thanks to this observation that we can make of ourselves, we come to find some answers about many things that we do not understand; we can reach the "true knowledge", which can only be found within us; we can come to understand how we really function, towards what direction we are heading and know if this is the right one or not.

We only acquire that wisdom if we place ourselves above the limitations of our own mind, if we reach that space where we find ourselves, that "center" where we stop being asleep, which is in a somewhat deeper place that we can discover if we go through the silence and observe the stillness of our own mind.

From there we access a beautiful world, which is not dominated by the imagination or by those constant and repetitive thoughts that arise in our mind. From there we can make great discoveries about ourselves, acquiring the truth of everything that surrounds us.

It is a way of detaching from the world to understand ourselves much better and to be able to understand and resolve all those questions that we encounter along the way, which we do not know how to decipher immediately but which are kept in the depths of our memory, waiting for the moment to be resolved.

We find it difficult to manifest

In general, we find it difficult to manifest those things that are located in the deepest part of our inner world. We tend to make the decision to silence them, because we think that in this way we protect ourselves.

Therefore, when we extract information about ourselves, we do not take advantage of it to make it known, we do not get rid of it, we do not manifest it outside, to the people around us.

We somehow separate everything that is in our inner world from the external world. We do not express many things that we carry inside, even if we are rushing into an abyss or we feel disturbed, or we do not find enough balance to settle our affairs or all those inconveniences that are exposed before us on a daily basis, facing the outside.

We continue to maintain our composure as if nothing is hurting us; we continue with the determination to continue acting as if everything was understandable to us and we do not have to hide anything, any inner conflict or any other problem that is being represented in our mind at that moment; although internally we live in a world full of setbacks.

The truth is that outwardly we hide it very well. There are many people who seem to radiate happiness, but deep inside themselves there is a disenchantment that is dazing them in a dominant anguish.

We do not want those around us to mistrust us, and that is why we always try to show ourselves as confident people, with a balanced life and reasonable judgments, so we always seek to omit any dark element that is stirring us up and messing us up inside.

We try to give an image of calmness to others. We do not want to appear as weak beings who are not capable of finding solutions; rather we prefer to hide and pretend through a false image that which we are not.

We are not able to free ourselves from our own mental disorder, we prefer to keep it in silence; although externally we live in a fiction that has nothing to do with what we really feel, deep down inside ourselves.

Benefits

To approach such knowledge we must accept that in our inner world there is a space where we meet ourselves and access information that has to do with what we are, that brings us closer to the true understanding of all our past experiences.

If we walk this path we will immerse ourselves through calmness in our spiritual part, which is far from thoughts and the whim of the imagination. In such a state there are no contradictions, no unconscious impulses or images arising from our memory to interrupt us or shift our attention to other, more distant contents.

If over time we prolong our stay in this environment and take advantage of all the knowledge we find in it, we will bring out the best in ourselves, free ourselves in some way from the bonds of the mind and enhance our best abilities: those that are attached to what we really are, that we only get to know if we access that hidden and secret space that is apparently hidden, beyond our own thoughts, at a higher level of consciousness that we can only access if we reduce all that mental noise that stops us and imprisons us constantly, without daring to take a step further.

All this will enrich us, because it will increase our knowledge of the world and of ourselves, which will help us when facing daily difficulties; when looking for solutions to each of those problems to which we are subject, which we often keep in time because we do not stop to listen to ourselves to try to find a way out and correct our own mistakes.

Thanks to our mental power we can achieve it, we can reduce the anguish and all that suffering created by our false beliefs, which are accompanied by a series of thoughts that try to dominate us.

Until we wake up we are not aware, in many occasions, of the confusion that is inside ourselves, of everything that is contributing to live in a permanent agitation, that seems that never descends, that is always increasing, submerging us in an abyss of obstacles loaded with impediments that are mixed one with another until we do not manage to find a way out.

The key is to persist, to never deviate from that "center" that is within you and that is permanent; where you find true understanding, order and enough tranquility to be able to move away from the deception of the mind and all that restless suffering that abounds in many thoughts of the past.

6. The power of reality

Sometimes, we dress everything in a disguise that is not the real one, to justify ourselves or to extract from an event only what is convenient for us.

The fact is that we always use every experience we observe to our advantage. We reduce everything to what interests us at any given moment, and we forget what everything really is.

If we live asleep, under the influence of our own thoughts, we will be subjected to everything that happens in the mind.

Everything that circulates and moves in it is propagated until it is transferred to our conducts and behaviors, to what we do in our daily life.

If we abandon our attention and do not observe in depth all this, we will live determined by all these elements that arise in our own mind. They will become established in us, spreading throughout our consciousness, and will manage to dominate us completely.

In the end, we will observe a reality created by our own mind through all these processes. It may be that in some moments it is a false reality, since it has been created on the basis of contents that have a similarity but that we have not previously analyzed; we have created it from automatic expressions that have emerged from our unconscious because they were already stored in our memory.

We can create a fiction, an illusion from the union of fragments of contents that have a certain relationship. In such a way that we can submerge ourselves in a fantasy created through our own imagination, in a false reality that can take hold of us at the same time that we are enlarging it and accommodating ourselves to it.

Their movements are very fast and they always try to build new content structures and create images that can confuse us and even change our own reasoning.

Sometimes, our main difficulties come from there, from an accumulation of ideas and indeterminate thoughts that separate us from the truth of things and lead us down a disorderly path that isolates us from the world; that inclines us to deviate from our "true purpose", creating in us a false, improper world, where we submerge ourselves in an unconscious way, renouncing our own will to establish another way of acting more conscious, more prone to reflection and more useful to our true desires.

We simply let ourselves be carried away obediently by any idea from the first moment it manifests itself in our consciousness, and we give up, we give up what we should really do; and we remain attached to that thought that has been introduced in our mind in an unconscious way, without any explanation, that little by little is separating us from ourselves, from that space that is also inside us and that we can only perceive through meditation and calmness.

INVENTED REALITY

Sometimes our mind creates a false world for us and we stubbornly remain in it, because somehow we are interested in living there, resting in an ideal world, invented, where we do not go through any difficulty or problems exist.

A fantastic world where everything is already written in advance; where everything goes according to plan and you feel protected and all are advantages and you do not have to fight or deal with the present, with the world and with all those external circumstances that usually dominate the context in which you live and to which you have to adapt if you want to maintain a link with real life.

All the inventions and fantasies that you come to create in your mind, are contents that arise from your memory that come together, sometimes without any reflection on your part, until they totally invade your consciousness and align themselves, creating a structure of thoughts that eventually begin to exert their dominion over you.

Everything that is created in your mind influences your own happiness. Everything that is articulated in your consciousness becomes arguments, concepts that carve your own personality, that incline you to think in a certain way.

The contents that are developed in this kind of processes can sometimes hit us with fantasies far away from reasonableness. If we follow them without considering the consequences, they can harm us, since they are representations that appear in our conscience without our having reasoned them conveniently, and in addition they arise in an automatic way.

In those moments we allow ourselves to be fascinated by them and we begin to walk in the direction that they mark us. After a while we become aware of our mistake, that it has been a mistake on our part to let ourselves be subordinated by this automatic mechanism that has not allowed us to properly evaluate those thoughts that have occupied our consciousness, and to which we have not given them the importance they deserved.

Many times we live in a delirium that does not stop, that alters us completely, providing us with a contamination in our thoughts that excludes us from reality; in such a way that in the end we fall off the cliff, we are completely wrong.

We are content to follow the current, without further ado, of all those inventions that are created without any foundation, that agglutinate in our mind in such a way that they lead us to ignore the reality that surrounds us.

Sometimes, we degrade ourselves in our own darkness, even if it is not pleasant for us. We like to accumulate fictions, mirages that separate us from reality and distract us, that immobilize us, since they do not help us to distinguish what is truly important to us.

We destroy ourselves, many times, due to the disturbances and the enormous upheavals that we create and feed in our own mind.

Disconnecting from reality

Most of them are inventions created to disconnect from reality, to separate us from the world, because in it we find a permanent disappointment and we try to deceive ourselves by escaping to another disguised reality.

It is a way to escape from the misfortunes of life, a way to abandon the real world and all those daily worries that affect us.

Many times we give up facing life because we are overcome by discouragement and we lose our balance and our level of resistance to anguish and confusion drops.

In this way we end up detaching ourselves from reality, evoking another much friendlier world, free of disturbances and away from suffering, where we can go without any anguish; without any problem that extends over time, without anything affecting us.

It is a way of hiding from the world, keeping ourselves busy with other things that make us forget reality at every moment. It is a way to evaporate from the worries, from the inconveniences that are part of life and that we cannot omit so easily, because they will always be there, even if we do not want them to be.

Sometimes we destroy ourselves, creating other worlds to find a satisfaction that we do not find in the present, in our daily life.

We try to look for happiness and well-being, although with time we realize that this is not the best alternative -trying to solve problems by running away from them-, that the best way to stop all suffering and the restlessness that dominates us is to stay "awake"; to make better use of our reasoning and use all these tools to face each and every one of life's inconveniences, to disintegrate all that affliction that has been growing in us slowly, for not knowing how to make the right decisions at the right time.

If we separate ourselves from the world and associate our thoughts to an invented reality, a division will be created within us that will gradually split us apart. We will be totally disconnected from what we are, trying to escape to other alternatives created by our own thoughts, following the current of all those images that arise without any explanation in our mind.

INACCURATE JUDGMENTS

We may register a lot of information in an imprecise way, we may remain chained to an incorrect interpretation of reality, we may cover up the truth of things with a layer of falsehood. We may not be as transparent as we appear to be; sometimes our ingenuity shapes reality to our liking.

In the end, we limit ourselves to observing things from our point of view. We transform what we see to make it understandable, even if we reach some conclusions that are not true.

We always place ourselves in the position that is most convenient for us, even if it is often not the correct one.

Often, our conclusions are the result of unconvincing beliefs that we nurture through a series of inaccurate judgments that we have consolidated over time.

In many moments the inner narration of the events that happen to us is not entirely accurate: many times it obeys ridiculous impressions that we deposit in our memory and that do not correspond to the truth, to reality.

We do not always judge objectively what is manifested before us, we simply keep the least important of things, with the most perishable details, and we dissociate ourselves from the background, from the true meaning they have.

Many times we contribute, without being very conscious of it, to increase our confusion. We do not try to solve that which we do not understand, nor do we reflect on it, nor do we look for the truth of things and we do not care to know if our reasoning is true or not.

BELIEFS

We remain with the same ideas for long periods of time. We develop them, adding new arguments to them, using new terms to refer to the same thing.

We support them in some way; in such a way that with the passage of time they take on a greater dimension until they begin to influence our own decisions, and they become established in our reasoning and determine our beliefs.

Sometimes, we have a delirious vision of everything that happens to us. We are slaves, in a way, of all that information stored in our memory, which sometimes builds wrong beliefs about the world and who we are.

Many of these beliefs separate us from reality in some cases, they take us away from common sense and upset us, spreading through our mind in an unrestrained way; while we keep feeding them, without getting out of that chaos that is breaking us inside, without rest.

In the end, we incorporate them into our own mental structure, in such a way that they end up influencing our way of seeing the world and everything that happens to us.

It is there where we elaborate our beliefs, which are actually the result of the union of a series of thoughts that we have been nurturing over time on a particular subject.

Sometimes they are reproduced in our mind without stopping, they remain in our memory and we cannot release them so easily.

They can dominate our consciousness if we allow it. If not, they spread further and shape our thoughts and judgments and opinions about everything that happens to us.

Once they are established within us, they last in time, until circumstances or some life experience make us change them for others more convenient.

If we do not take care of them, with the passing of the years they resist to disappear. So we remain with the same approaches for long periods of time, so that we do not abandon them so easily; although sometimes we have doubts, we persevere in the same opinions and in the same way of interpreting the world and everything that surrounds us.

If we allow it, we will allow ourselves to be led by them and by all that mental movement that little by little takes over us, guiding us and leading us, sometimes in the wrong direction.

It is not so easy to destroy our beliefs, even if we realize that they are wrong, it is not so easy to change them for others. Once all these ideas have spread through our mind, even if we later reflect on them, they become strong within us, they join a structure of thoughts that we can hardly move; and even if we examine it again and again, we do not find the way to apply the necessary changes to achieve another vision, another new perspective of what surrounds us.

How to free ourselves from them

Our true liberation occurs when we do not allow ourselves to be seduced by all those ideas and false beliefs that we accumulate and to which we obey and submit and allow them to direct us in an incomprehensible way; even though we do not see any reward in them.

We are really free when we are conscious of that movement in which all those elements that rush into our mind and activate us in such a way that we put all our attention on them.

When we clean our mind of all that we are also using our mental power; we are clarifying our consciousness so that it takes us to a balance that makes us grow, that changes our intentions and that takes us to actions that manifest what we really are; that are related to our true inner purpose.

If we increase our attention on all that is distributed in our mind, we protect ourselves from the deception of thoughts, which sometimes alter us with impressions that lead us to anguish, to gloom, to despondency.

We must be attentive to everything that settles in it, since it will alter us; it will modify our actions. We must be sure to follow only that which is in our favor. We cannot allow our life to be a bewilderment, that we circulate around without a determined direction; that we become obsessed with maintaining an ignorant life, without activity, totally opposed to what we really are, full of contradictions and incoherencies.

For this we must look at the constant chattering that we have within ourselves and that is caused by all those thoughts that we incorporate and that are chained with each other; and that over time are settling with our consent, without us judging whether they are good or bad.

These thoughts grow, they take over our reason, and sometimes they fill us with contradictions that get involved with each other until they produce an internal disorder that distances us from reality, from the truth.

All this is important to keep in mind if we want to improve this process, if we want to avoid the influence in our mind of those contents that oppress us, that go deep within ourselves and that disconcert us without rest, with impressions on which we do not have time to reflect, because they ascend and descend very quickly throughout the length and breadth of our own consciousness, without hardly having time to observe their movements.

When we cannot separate ourselves from them, it is possible to observe them from calmness and realize how we have created them; on what principles they are based and how they influence our reasoning and appear in our inner discourse.

Our mental power gives us this possibility to inquire into our inner world; to observe some elements and see how we create our own interpretations. Then we will have the opportunity to make some changes and thus diminish their influence.

We have before us a great task: Which is to be above this mental dimension, where thoughts increase and distract us and separate us from what we are, while little by little we begin to feel smaller and smaller, more and more insignificant, and in the end we do not manage to be ourselves, before the increase of all those thoughts that are changing us, transforming us, without us hardly intervening; that are introducing us in an enigmatic world, where nothing adjusts to reality and there are only contradictions that then become beliefs that lead us to failure, to a permanent and useless frustration.

IMAGINATION

When our imagination rises, it convinces us with illusory beliefs that it invents to falsify the truth, to alter the vision of the facts; in such a way that it manages to establish in us a series of misguided impressions that, in the end, separate us from reality, since they are neither clear, nor firm, nor defined.

Our imagination takes hold of us and creates in our conscience a series of impressions that guide us, unless we examine them and realize that we are under an automatic procedure that does not stop and that tries to dominate us if we do not remedy it.

There are moments in which it is necessary that your imagination is present, that we imagine a better world and that we fight to establish it. Sometimes, it is like a necessary seed for us to be convinced that there are some things that are possible, and therefore it is worth trying and fighting for them.

In this sense, imagination is a kind of suggestion for us: we come to feel convinced that some goals will be realized if we have previously imagined them in our own mind.

To find the power of your mind is to make proper use of your own imagination, to become aware that it can make you believe in a fantastic world, far from reality; although it is also an essential tool to foster your own creativity, to imagine and visualize your goals before undertaking them.

Your true mental power lies in knowing how to distinguish what is real from what is unreal; to discern what is only imagination from what is not.

It is essential that we pay attention to all those ideas that are propagated through our own imagination and that incline us, without us being very conscious of it, to see reality in a specific way; many times without following a reasonable logic.

They tend to be contents that we cannot easily remove and that repeat themselves in that room that is our conscience, trying to take us in a direction that ends up isolating us from what we should really do to be coherent with ourselves.

Reality is in your own consciousness, you can clearly distinguish it when you observe the activity that is in it and you stop and learn to separate the contents and to pause all that mental movement that absorbs you and plunges you into unconsciousness, that makes you live submerged in a deep sleep in which you can remain for a long time, without hardly giving you time to observe what is happening inside you and that little by little is turning you into an indifferent robot.

LEAVING THE FICTION

Sometimes, there can be an abyss within ourselves that disunites us from what we are and forces us to live in a delirium that little by little is being designed in our mind, without us being very aware of it; it can spread and extend in time.

To eliminate it, we must know where it originates that kind of thoughts that have led us to invent a series of ideas that in reality are nothing more than artifices contrary to the truth; that we have been inventing to mask reality, because they are irrational and absurd, although they are scattered throughout our mind, installed in the deepest part of ourselves.

So we must move away from them, omit them, disregard them; then they will begin to drift away and we will forget to observe them and they will stop multiplying in our consciousness.

We live enchanted in our mental disorder, ignoring the consequences that this entails. We stubbornly go forward, many times, without a fixed course, without thinking about where we are going.

Therefore, it is important that we realize the transcendence of all those thoughts that we keep in time and that are repeated over and over again creating another vision of the world.

In these cases it becomes necessary that we orient the direction, the sense of our thoughts; that we appease all that mental noise that entangles us and encloses us in a world of repetitive contents that occupy all the immensity of our conscience.

In this way we can get to the origin of everything that happens; we can build a new reality much more settled, closer to the truth. We will reach knowledge and abandon the darkness in which we are often submerged by our own imagination, which forces us to create a deceitful character that does not stop to think and lives in an unreal world, driven by its own contradictions.

Our mind also has this power, if we do not use it properly. If we are inclined to pay attention and observe its functioning, we will not allow ourselves to be conditioned, we will not live under its deception.

If we are aware that everything we do is initiated in this realm, in this territory, then we can free ourselves from this uncertain mechanism that decides for us and that we accept without further ado.

With a little willpower on our part, we can conquer our inner space and somehow fix our vision of reality, some of our beliefs and all those wrong interpretations of some past experiences.

We cannot escape from that which dominates us inside, which corrupts us and complicates our existence. For this we can use reflection, to prevent all those inventions of our imagination that entangle us in a frantic way, irradiating in us doubt, indecision and a restlessness that little by little is tormenting us.

We will realize that many times it tries to captivate us with thoughts that lead us to another reality different from the existing one.

All this can be done from temperance, when we do not allow ourselves to be contaminated by this constant movement of the mind, which is permanently active and is always proposing something to us.

Achieving clarity

If we ignore all this that happens inside, we will forget ourselves; we will live in an illusory life, contaminated by all the thoughts that are produced in our mind, because we will live under its influence; we will let ourselves be carried away by all those ideas that are impregnated in our conscience and that in many occasions manifest themselves without us provoking them, pushing us to act in a way far away from what our principles are and from what we should do to be ourselves at all times.

If we go into the depths of our inner world, we can draw all these conclusions; and we can even intervene to remove ourselves from the influence exerted by our own mind, when we are indifferent and do not guess the consequences of acting in an unconscious way, without perceiving the true reality of what surrounds us, without exploring ourselves from the serenity.

We must achieve "clarity", guess, anticipate all these processes that spread through our consciousness and that are destroying what we are, because they are molding us in an unconscious way, run over, while we remain submissive, obedient, as if hiding behind all this maelstrom of thoughts that we are constantly feeding; that are appearing again and again from the depths of our memory, moving us to other worlds, to another reality that is moving us away from the real one, from "what is".

Mental power

Your mental power is also found, in some way, in observing how all those thoughts transport you to another reality, to another way of understanding the world; in perceiving how many times you remain immobile, without being able to reason, when a mistaken belief suppresses your own illusions and condemns you to live a life full of uncertainties, without certainties, while inside you an inner dialogue is established in which a restlessness is diffused that little by little is increasing and ends up turning your consciousness into a conflict that entangles you very easily.

When we use our mental power, we can perceive and experience all this that occurs within us, which can help us to stop living in fiction; to leave aside all those thoughts that intoxicate us, that are confusing and that make us have an inaccurate vision of reality.

Our mental power lies in knowing how to suppress, diminish, all that subjugation, that constant mechanism that contaminates us little by little and that leaves a trace in our memory; that leads us to useless behaviors.

It enables you to have the ability to replace all those illusory images that sometimes flood your own imagination, creating a new reality far from common sense. In such a way that it allows you to return to mental logic, which dissolves all those confusions created in your consciousness, which at the beginning are silent, but with time they take presence in your mind until they take over your own reason.

If you want to use your mental power, you have to glimpse all those contents that appear in your mind and that try to mold you, to submerge you in another reality that is less boring but more distant from the truth. You must not allow these contents to accumulate and concentrate, originating new thought structures that lead you to transform your way of seeing the world.

If we use our mental power properly, we can grow, we can be above all that cerebral excitement; we can move away from confusion and begin to understand everything that manifests within ourselves.

7. The power of order

Your mental power allows you to establish order within your inner world; to organize the elements that arise in your mind and to achieve a certain control over all those impulses that arise, sometimes without explanation, and which you do not usually resist.

In fact, our true mental power is based on this, on the capacity to put back in order that which appears disordered, which many times we do not examine with sufficient tranquility, because we are thoughtless and our own nature leads us to pursue the irrational, to persevere in acting in an involuntary way, without a stable purpose that determines us.

We all have this quality that belongs to our mental power; although not all of us use it, due to lack of knowledge, lack of interest or simply because we do not consider it necessary.

It is a power that remains in us, even if we do not make use of it. We can only identify it when we observe ourselves and try to go a little deeper into that which is not seen.

We have something extraordinary inside; it is hidden and we can discover it when we need to transform ourselves. It can help us to achieve the balance, order and clarity necessary to face the deception of our own thoughts.

INTERNAL DISORDER

Everything we experience, everything that affects us in some way, depends on the use of the mind; on everything that is reproduced there, in that gear that we constantly feed with elements of the past, of our history, that are intertwined without order in all that immense space where all the traces that we have printed in our memory are diffused.

Your mind is a flow of ideas that divide you inside, that divert your attention elsewhere, towards a quantity of unnecessary stimuli that the only thing they do is to mess up even more your own confusion, which you can sometimes feel.

In our mind everything appears disordered, all those representations that are never exhausted and that you visualize, while they appear in your consciousness in a confusing way, wasting your energy and making you interpret reality in a certain way.

Our mind, in reality, is a combination of processes of a great activity that occupy an extensive space and that regularly appear disordered, although there is a constant combination of similar contents.

They can maintain a certain direction and in a short space of time they can take the opposite path; that is why we can pass, for example, from joy to sadness very quickly.

Therefore, we must be very aware of everything that is represented in our mind, since it can contribute to sow an internal discrepancy that leads us to conflict and to a series of dissonant reasonings that separate us from the truth and objectivity of things.

Conflicts, when they are internal, spread inside, creating disorder and division that you cannot mask. Your contrariness is something that is easily observable. It grows inside you, sometimes irrationally, and separates you from common sense.

Then you begin to see things in an imprecise way, because you are moving away from reason, you are not able to distinguish the truth, you are subordinated to your own problems without being able to hide it.

Confusion

Sometimes you do not find yourself, you walk distracted in the abandonment; your disordered mind transports you towards a confusion in which you accommodate yourself and you do not try to fix it, on the contrary: you protect it and you reinforce it by habituating yourself to it, gathering more thoughts that join the previous ones with urgency.

In the end, you live as absent, attached to some beliefs that you have been adding and have been appropriated by hypnotizing you.

In reality, this is what divides us inside, when we allow ourselves to be captivated by the fascination of some stupefying thoughts that grow inside us, pushing us to live in a confusion that we unconsciously reinforce.

Setbacks cause us to expend a lot of energy. If we do not have the skill to fix in time that which causes us affliction, to free ourselves from what limits us, an attitude will be installed that little by little will lead us to a permanent alteration.

In such a situation, it is easy for anguish to take hold of us; that we get stuck, that we tire easily; that we feel more and more irritated.

In those moments is when we begin to experience a sensation that strangles us inside, that discourages us, obfuscating us, with increasing intensity; until it begins to emanate, from the deepest part of ourselves, a disorder that disturbs our own reason, that makes us lethargic, that inclines us to a way of thinking close to pessimism, to a sad approach to life.

It is evident that what makes us despair is found within ourselves, as well as everything that diminishes and restricts us. All that is sustained and consolidated in our own mind; it is there where it is supported and takes strength.

All the unconscious processes that are projected inside you, do it continuously. Sometimes they have so much influence over you that they can make you live in the most absolute darkness, so that you do not become aware of the consequences of certain ideas taking hold of you and becoming behaviors that influence your way of proceeding.

It is easy to notice the signs that appear both outside and inside ourselves, to know if we lead a satisfactory life; or if we are somewhat lost, far from "what we are", in a sphere of confusion that makes us live in a permanent deception.

We remain in disorder

We can allow all this to happen if we turn our attention away from what is happening in our own mind and run away through pastimes and entertainments that do not allow us to grasp what is happening within ourselves.

We insist on remaining in the internal disorder and we do not try to appease that noise that rises and that angers us inside and that directs us in a tenacious way; even though we feel uncomfortable and we know that we are heading towards a precipice, that we are going in a direction contrary to the one we should be going.

Many times we are indifferent to our own confusion, that which corrupts us from within, which supplies us with negative thoughts that are annihilating us in a confusion that leads us to have an erroneous vision of life.

Many times we make a mistake when we put our focus of attention, we do not pay attention to what may be causing confusion in us; to those ideas or beliefs that may be irrational and that we do not reject or suppress; we simply allow them to remain there, integrated in our mind. We do not mind that they disturb us and disrupt our vision of reality.

If we do not sort ourselves out inside, we will not be rational, we will overlook the deception to which we are subjected, living according to the limiting impulses of our own mind.

We only realize it when we see the consequences of our mental imbalance; we see that there is an inner disorder that disturbs us and that we have neglected it for a while, abandoning ourselves to an irrational mode of existence that has separated us from the world around us.

Sometimes, this time can be excessive and can lead us to a more prolonged isolation, which we do not manage to stop if we do not take care to clear up that disorder that at those moments has unfolded within us and that is deteriorating us in some way.

In such a way that in the end we get used to live in internal disorder, losing part of our freedom, letting our mind take control and establish what has to be done in each moment. We do not dare to face that endless train of unconscious and impulsive contents that agitate and confuse us.

TO PUT THE MIND IN ORDER

Wherever you go, your inner conflicts will also be there, they will always accompany you. The only way to stop them is to expel them from your own mind, with willingness.

We must annihilate that which disturbs us. We cannot live disoriented, without knowing who we are. We have to get away from the daze, from everything that separates us from ourselves, so it is necessary that we distinguish what produces stagnation, what keeps us in a permanent irritation, in restlessness or disorder.

We have to learn to suppress everything that fractures us inside. If we do so, we will be truly utilizing our true mental power. We cannot allow that within us there is a disorder that makes us live separated from "what we are".

We have to know that everything is grouped there, in our mind, in that space where we ourselves create the difficulties and an unfounded disorder that can keep sinking us until we are totally paralyzed, not knowing what to do.

If we do not use it properly and do not use its true power, it can lead us astray. If we do not use our reasoning to properly analyze all those representations that appear in it, we can fall into bewilderment, into mental disorder, into error.

We have to remind ourselves that we are what we think, that all our mistakes come from an internal disorder, from an irrational way of seeing things, from wrong interpretations of the reality we observe outside.

We must be prepared so that this does not occur, so it is necessary that we know well this mental mechanism that often pushes us out of reality and stuns us and does not disconnect us from the world and prevents us from acting in the way that deep down we consider to be the most appropriate for us.

He who uses his mental power is interested in untangling this inner disorder, until he manages to establish balance again; then he appreciates tranquility again, when he discovers that what was destroying him begins to purify itself.

Paying attention

When we feel that there is disorder, we must calm down and pay attention to that which is increasing our restlessness; it is the only way to find out what is causing us discomfort.

When we feel that there is some kind of disturbance, we must pay attention to what is causing it. We have to evaluate, in some way, the cause of that which is bothering us, of that which is making us experience an uneasiness that can immobilize us, that can prevent us from moving forward in a serene way.

It is necessary that we look inside ourselves and that we get used to observe all those irrational and confused thoughts that lead us to obtain a wrong vision of reality.

We must always try to look for an accessible way out of all the difficulties we encounter, both outside and inside ourselves.

The only way to do this is through a conscious look, by which we put all our attention on all the things that are happening. This is the only way to determine a solution and to find a rational explanation for all that we are observing.

With practice, it will not cost us any effort to fix this mechanism that will help us to order our ideas a little better.

In reality, everything depends on our approaches, on the care we take to notice those irrational ideas that often come to us and that move uncontrollably through our consciousness.

We only have to pay attention to what happens inside us, to all those representations that we observe in our mind, that unite with others and never seem to be diluted, that never disappear, repeating themselves over and over again, creating a false interpretation of everything that happens to us: of all those experiences that we have every day, about which we make our own conjectures, sometimes mistaken.

It is necessary that you go deep into all those mental representations that harm you. In this way you will be able to change direction, remaining indifferent to those contents. You will see that with time they will begin to weaken, as they will cease to be useful and will slowly disappear.

We must pay the utmost attention to our judgments; they may not be very sensible sometimes. They create impressions in us that then leave an imprint that develops until it extorts reality.

We may give relevance to certain reasonings that have no logical explanation, we simply let them take over and lead us to definite conclusions that in the end permanently distort reality.

Observing the internal dialogue

When you keep your attention within yourself, you can clearly observe your internal dialogue, how it is installed in you a speech that you repeat frequently, sometimes in a hasty manner, and that changes over the course of time.

This inner talk sometimes disturbs you, and at other times it leads you to calm, but you always end up repeating the same arguments, to the point that they come to dominate you, thus occupying almost all the space of your consciousness.

Depending on the attention you pay to them, they can increase or decrease; they increase if it is an issue that affects you for some reason.

When we feel some kind of internal discomfort, at a mental level, we should not hesitate to use our attention to open an interval that allows us to moderate that inner dialogue that may be leading us down a path with possible negative consequences for us.

Observing all this teaches you to separate those contents that are not really interesting for you, that do not fit what really matters; it is a way to use your mental power as well.

You will begin to experience a greater strength, which you discern in a different, more confident way, highlighting the positive in you; through your inner dialogue, in which you begin to encourage yourself and find a little more objectivity in things.

Managing content

Before obeying our own mind and everything that is established there, we must learn to manage its contents, its influence, being aware of the importance that thoughts have in all our actions; in what we repeat automatically.

Everything that happens in our mind is very powerful. It can benefit us or lead us to a permanent dissatisfaction; it depends on how we manage all those thoughts that dominate us, on how we orient all those contents that appear in our conscience and that feed our ideas and our beliefs; sometimes false, because we elaborate them in an automatic way, without order, so that they lead us to a deception that we can only distinguish with time, when we see that confusion takes hold of us.

Therefore, it is important the way we have of ordering the components of our own mental mechanism: of all those elements that form its structure.

If they are related to contents that diminish our capacities, we will not be able to make use of our mental power, we will not have the opportunity to benefit from it; if, on the contrary, we know how to diminish all those toxic contents that are inserted in our mind, in an unconscious way, and that are introduced in our ways of thinking, affecting our reason, we will be able to fully employ all our mental functions, in such a way that all the best that is in us will occupy the center of our own consciousness.

This is the best way to re-establish order within you. If you do not act, if you do not take control and select what is truly important, you will live in slavery to the difficulties and obstacles that your mind continually proposes to you.

This possibility of putting aside those things that do not make much sense, that are limiting you, somehow makes your conscience to flatten, not to be subjected to that constant yoke of thoughts that drown you and weaken you, turning off your "inner calm".

If we do not establish a structure, they can lead us to disorder, because many thoughts arise and build themselves with an unusual frequency, without any opposition from us. We simply let them articulate themselves, even if some of them disturb us and lead us to bewilderment or isolate us from reality; we are unconcerned about them, allowing them to lead us to disorder, while we remain attentive to other kinds of things.

When we move all these contents to one side, our mind returns to order, thoughts stop circulating without sense and you begin to see how everything is flooded with an inner peace that makes you wake up and separate you from that mental dream in which you remain asleep most of the time; then you begin to feel the calm, which has always lived in you, what happens is that you can not appreciate it because of the agitation that is in your mind.

We just have to get away from all that maelstrom of contents that prevent our own transformation, that block our development and that, if we do not avoid it, determine us unconsciously in everything we do.

The importance of meditation

It is good to practice meditation -you will also be using, in this sense, your mental power-, to clear your mind, so as not to allow problems to corner you and in the end you will be overwhelmed by all those negative thoughts that arise in an active and powerful way.

First you must detect them, if you want to get your ideas on track, and then you have to detach yourself from them by letting them pass. Then they will have no effect on you, they will become small and your view of things will begin to improve.

In a way it also serves us to calm anxiety; it is a way to eliminate our unconscious impulses, which in many occasions mobilize us making us act in an undesired, opposite direction.

In this sense, your mental power lies in the ability to appease all that mental noise that expands within you, without any control, throughout the length and breadth of your consciousness.

If we give the mind the importance it deserves, we will transform it into a pleasant place, into an environment that provides us with the right state of mind to build ourselves in the best possible way, so that we do not live in a permanent division that distances us from "what we are", that alters us inside and leads us to live an unhappy, incomplete life, and detached from our own reality.

If we use our mental power, we can fight against unhappiness, against that discouragement, often permanent and disproportionate, which slowly distresses us, spreading throughout our inner world until it leads us to a continuous worry.

It is about always having a balance in everything we do and stop being subordinated to that mental madness in which we often remain; in which we allow ourselves to be imprisoned by a series of thoughts that guide us in a certain direction.

We must also extend our vision within ourselves, to definitively put an end to everything that confuses us; that unbalances us; that makes us unbalanced, weakening us, leading us to permanent failure, to live a confused and diverse life, without a specific interest; abandoned to the fate of what our mind dictates at any given moment.

Getting out of confusion

When everything is annulled inside, you must not allow confusion to dominate you. You must try to clarify everything that is affecting you; and of course not to magnify it.

We must separate ourselves from everything that produces an alteration. If we encounter any setback or have confusing thoughts, we must clarify our mind by separating all those harmful contents that make us unhappy and lead us to behaviors that are inconsistent with who we really are.

It is advisable that we try to find an explanation to all that manifests itself in our conscience; to establish an order in all that exhibition of data that appears before us and that is transmitted permanently and without any limitation.

Our mental power is also based on noticing the deception that is hidden behind all that activity. If we are aware and manage this mechanism, we can set aside those elements that are useless for our purposes. In this way we can reestablish a mental order that will help us to come out of the darkness in which we are sometimes immersed.

We should not be guided by the traps of our mind, although many times we allow ourselves to be impressed by what we see in our consciousness, which shows itself to us in such a way that it traps us and leads us in another direction.

Our mental power can help us out of confusion, out of darkness. It can protect us from negativity, which is often activated when a sharp impulse is ignited within us that takes possession of us and leads us to hold in our mind only that which disturbs us, that diminishes us, that corrupts us.

Thanks to our mental power we can discover what it is that leads us to confusion, what brings us closer to disorder.

We can stop being affected by all those disturbances that rise up inside us, that agglomerate and make us live a gloomy life.

If we are content to live in disorder and we do not pay attention to that which blocks our will, we will hardly be able to think for ourselves; it will be an automatic mental mechanism that will do it for us.

It is possible to improve ourselves if we interrupt those vicious circles in which we are sometimes immersed and which we lengthen in time, without considering the consequences they are having for us.

It depends on our will, on persevering and not escaping. It depends on us not to live in that huge disorder that sometimes exists inside and that slowly shrinks us, disuniting us, suspending any glimpse of illusion and hope.

You will discover your authentic path and all that disturbs you and leads you to confusion, that tries to direct you. You will know how to place it in its exact place, so that it does not disorient you; in those moments you will know the causes of everything that has led you to "be what you are".

8. The power of calm

He who uses his mental power must always have the purpose of finding calm, in the midst of all that agitation that often exists within our inner world; that is why he must know how to explore all that space that is often kept hidden, where all those thoughts that maintain an activity for a long time and that move without ceasing throughout the length and breadth of our consciousness begin to emerge and strengthen.

In this case, your mental power is based on the knowledge of all those mechanisms that are required to reach that "inner calm" in which you distance yourself in some way from the influence of external stimuli and also from the mental noise caused by your own thoughts.

STATE OF STILLNESS

This "inner calm" allows you to have this vision always, and when you reach this state of stillness, away from everything that can distract

you at that moment, it is a way to go a little further, a way to discover what is behind the normal
processes of the mind.

The good use, in this case, of our mental power, can also lead us to find calm among all that
internal noise that we sometimes feel.

You get it when you diminish all that exaltation that you sometimes feel when a set of
thoughts pile up that do not stop and try to dominate you. If you have the ability to lessen their
strength and do not let yourself be stunned, you
will be able to reach stillness: an inner calm that
will take you away from the power of those
thoughts that try to conquer you.

If we look carefully within ourselves, in addition to discovering what we are, we will also find
the way to find stillness: that tranquility that takes us away from anguish and from any disturbance invented by the very mechanisms of
thought, which sometimes entangle us and lead
us to a bewildering chaos.

Only if we perceive all this inner movement,
we can make use of our true mental power. We
will manage to find calm and tranquility when
necessary; far from the artifices of thought,
which slowly inclines us to make decisions that
end up sinking us into a false reality.

INNER PEACE

The power to find that inner peace is also a capacity that lies within you and that can remain hidden, hidden, if we do not use it or do not know it.

If you achieve this inner peace, you manage to enter a state of stillness from which you can observe yourself from a different perspective than the one you normally use; you can do it from a situation in which you observe everything that happens inside you from a privileged situation, from a position that allows you to establish a distance between what happens in your mind and yourself.

When you enter into a state of "inner peace", you somehow feel distanced from the usual mechanism of your own mind, so that you come to perceive everything in a more objective way, more detached from the usual normal influences, which usually interfere in our own vision of the reality of things.

Only if you find it and enter into this somewhat deeper dimension in you, you will realize that there are all these possibilities that do not exist in the external world, in the material world, in which you usually develop.

It will lead you to security, it will remove doubts and an inner glow will lead you to the conviction that this is the place where the truth and "what you really are" is.

If you are able to use your mental power properly, you will also find your "inner peace", which will take hold within you and lead you away from disorder and confusion. Little by little it will extend into your inner world, repairing any afflictions you feel.

THAT OTHER SPACE

When you manage to remove all these contents, you will immerse yourself in a void where nothing can distract you; you will separate yourself from all that activity and your attention will move to that other space, which also exists within you, where there is only silence and it is not contaminated by any form.

Your mental power can lead you to this movement, it can help you to move towards this place where there is only order and a stillness through which you can connect with your own being, with what you really are.

This would be the place where everything begins, where the true reason for all things rests, where there is no division and where you find the balance that resolves all difficulties, because it is far from the entanglements of thought and where "harmony" is reached, because there are no ideas, no beliefs or judgments that try to condition you or guide you in a certain direction.

Your mental power also enables you to move within your own consciousness to a higher level, where there are no images or objects and where you can observe everything as if you were a "witness", without being affected by anything.

It can place you in a privileged place where you reach the true understanding of things, because in that place is where the truth is, being away from the impressions of memory, from all those traces that we have been keeping through our own experiences and that sometimes contaminate our own vision of reality.

THE PAUSE

We can only reach understanding through the pause, which is a means to become aware of that which causes us suffering; the only way to enter that territory where our mind quiets down and we see everything in a clear, concrete way.

All manifestations appear less confused: all those impressions that are lodged in our mind that frequently reside in our consciousness, in an active form, that occupy our attention and that are constantly moving from one side to the other without stopping, without us preventing it.

They are fragments, similar contents, that are building within us a mental structure that, if we do not intervene, in some way is being elaborated automatically, unconsciously.

Sometimes, we are indifferent to this dynamic, we remain static before this process that is registered in our own mind. In such cases we allow ourselves to be infected by all those internal conflicts that we sometimes suffer, when some toxic thoughts burst in that we do not stop to examine and that influence our way of perceiving reality, of observing the world; in our way of reasoning...

When we ignore all this or we are indifferent, then we can find ourselves with a confusion that increases as all these thoughts are amplified, while they continue to manifest in our consciousness repeatedly.

If we pay attention to this mechanism and do not allow ourselves to be determined by our own mental contents, we will become stronger, more unshakable; we will not allow ourselves to be deceived and imprisoned by our own thoughts.

We will find the explanations to everything that happens to us; we will be present at all times, without feeding all those toxic contents that are always leaving a trace in our conscience that in the end ends up affecting us, in one way or another.

It is advisable not to submit to the dominion of our own mind. In this sense, we must show authority, maintain balance and not allow ourselves to be governed by all these processes that in the end manage to dominate us if we do not get ahead of them.

He who intends to use his mental power must act in this way, get used to consider that which is produced in our mind, anticipating everything that ends up influencing us, that inclines us to the execution of a series of habits that determine us and that do not stop until we are not aware and we are interested in the consequences that they may have for us.

The only way to stop all this frenetic activity is to move away, establishing a pause, and then we will find enough freedom to stop being captive of this internal and constant struggle that takes place in the deepest part of ourselves, and that is limiting us, stealing our peace, exterminating any initiative we may have to get to achieve what we really want.

THE SILENCE

To make an appropriate use of your mental power is to know how to take advantage of silence; to know the value it has; to understand that it is an essential tool to go deep inside ourselves.

Thanks to silence we can somehow stop the mental activity: all that incessant movement of continuous thoughts that exists within us and that does not stop if we do not stop it through tools such as meditation, observation, silence itself...

If we know how to use it correctly, we will have a very powerful tool to solve each and every one of the difficulties that life is posing us at every step, as it is a state that allows us to observe the circumstances, the situations from a more objective point of view and less contaminated by prejudices and by the whole set of ideas and irrational beliefs that often floods our mind, confusing our vision of things, and even our own judgments and reasoning.

If you really want to use all your mental power, you should not leave aside this tool that is "silence", because getting used to be in contact with it, is one of the essential requirements for the full development of your best qualities, of all those potentialities that are hidden in the depths of yourself and that you can not glimpse until you enter into that inner space freed from the bonds of the mind, through silence and calm.

If we immerse ourselves within our own inner self and observe all these processes from the calm, we will begin to find "harmony", which only ascends when we silence our mind and come into contact with serenity and silence and see how our own energy is transformed into an essential force that protects us, and that little by little leads us to stillness and to the path where our "true self" is found.

It leads us to control

Through silence we can experience our true mental power, since it helps us to take control of everything that happens in our consciousness.

Once we stop and do not allow any noise or any external influence to distract us, then we begin to take control of ourselves, of what is happening in our mind.

Just by pausing, there is this possibility that gives us great power; because, if we put it into practice, we can take control of ourselves, even of our own actions and behaviors.

It only depends on this, on knowing how to use silence, on knowing how to take advantage of all its richness that allows us, among other things, to enter into a space of stillness that leads us to the mastery of all those elements that exist in our inner world and that are in constant movement, conditioning us at every moment.

It facilitates the entrance to another dimension

Silence gives us an enormous power, because it is of great utility, since it facilitates the entrance to that other deeper dimension that is within ourselves, in which somehow we are freed from the bonds of all the repetitive and mechanical thoughts that occupy our mind.

Often, thanks to it, we can access that more spiritual dimension within us, which allows us to observe the world and reality in a more objective way, closer to the truth, with less prejudices and external influences.

Discovering all that emptiness, through silence, is a great discovery. It will be very useful, because in that place you are at a higher level of consciousness from which you have another perspective of all those contents that usually move in your mind and make you act in a way that often is not according to your "true self", to what deep inside yourself you would like to do; to lead a life in line with your "true purpose": with what you think you should do.

It is a dimension that can only be found within you, which can only be accessed through meditation, or from a state of tranquility, of calm, which can only be achieved through silence and away from everything that can distract you, from all those external influences that usually trap you and take you away from that "center" that is within you, but that remains hidden until you are aware of its existence and try to enter it to try to know yourself and discover many more things about yourself, about your own existence and about the world in which you live; your true mental power is there, in that space and in everything that happens in it.

9. The power of consciousness

He who is conscious of everything that springs up within himself and is exposed in his mind, can perfectly access the origin of all the things that have happened to him. He has the possibility of observing through the mental images that appear in his consciousness everything that has been his life: what has benefited him and what has harmed him; what has made him strong and what has led him to depression, to live in a diffuse fog where darkness settles and everything lacks meaning.

In this way, being conscious, we will obtain this kind of knowledge, we will be able to become aware of those mental contents that are toxic for us, that make us lose an immense amount of energy and time when we pay attention to them and stop doing those actions that we consider more appropriate for us.

In this way we will discover the way to direct our attention towards what certainly suits us; we will find the means to maintain a constant focus of attention on what really interests us, leaving aside all those useless thoughts that do not lead us anywhere and that are repeated over and over again arising in our consciousness impulsively, without us knowing how to stop them in many occasions.

When we are aware that this happens and we observe our thoughts that run through our mind in a repetitive and accelerated way, we realize those that are repeated more frequently, those that sooner or later lead us to a certain action.

Therefore, it is important to be aware that this process takes place within ourselves, and that its main elements are the thoughts and actions that we can carry out at a specific moment.

We will have the advantage of revealing our best qualities, our gifts; in short, our great mental power that we all have inside, but that we do not use because we remain impassive to this automatic movement of our mind that imposes an unconscious way of being, without us realizing it.

FINDING BALANCE

One always tries to find balance by trying to remain conscious, by embracing logical reasoning and trying to understand everything that happens. You always want to give up all those things that cause some kind of stridency; no one wants to sink and be crushed by the difficulties of life.

If you observe yourself and everything inside you, you will find balance and a way of communicating with yourself that you were unaware of before.

All this will lead you to cancel all those external influences, which are sometimes abundant, that you are continuously feeding on without realizing that you are subordinating yourself to everything that comes from the outside; that you are simply conforming to the information that comes from outside, leaving aside all that wisdom that is built within you, which you can only access if you get in touch with "what you are", in that center that is only reached through silence, when the noise of your mind is silenced and your thoughts stop acting and you begin to submit to a lucid, serene inner calm, through which you begin to perceive "what you really are", without anything can distract you.

WE CAN INTERVENE

Sometimes, everything is intermingled in our own mind: as soon as we are thinking about a certain subject, we are invaded by another kind of thoughts that have nothing to do with that subject; and later on, the first ones are repeated again and other different ones arise that have no relation with the previous ones.

It is a continuous wheel of images that seems to have no end, because we are incessantly looking for material in our memory to bring it to light gradually, repeatedly; all this through an unconscious mechanism that we hardly control, since it is part of our configuration.

In reality, our mental functioning is like this, by nature; although, if we are conscious, we can intervene and modify some parameters of this mechanism, because thanks to the internal observation of all these processes we can discover how they work, we can get to know them, we can become familiar with them, seeing at what point we can intervene so that this functioning is not so mechanical; so that it does not make us act like robots; to acquire a certain control over ourselves so that we do not have to depend so much on everything that is produced in our mind; to achieve in this way a certain degree of freedom that we can only get if we separate ourselves from this kind of conditioning, which often leads us to think and act without a clear sense; or even against ourselves, of what we think we should really do, but we do not do it because we unconsciously prefer to follow the guidelines that our own mind dictates to us, in an unconscious and automatic way.

We can only achieve this if we are aware of this mechanism, that this is taking place within ourselves and we manage to separate ourselves from it.

It is only possible to become aware of this functioning if we stop to observe how this process develops, if we are aware that this is constantly taking place within our own mind.

We can direct it if we are sufficiently aware of what is happening in it, of the processes that take place when we think about a particular subject or are performing a particular action.

Thanks to this exercise of consciousness that we can carry out within ourselves, we have the opportunity to discover how the mental mechanism works; and once we acquire this information we can then intervene to carry out a control and establish those modifications that we consider appropriate, especially to eliminate those habits with which we are not very happy and that have been taking hold of us, little by little, until they annul us completely on some occasions.

A NEW VISION OF THE WORLD

When you feel confused, do not give up on suppressing that detestable situation. Broaden your vision, go beyond and observe what is trying to dominate you. Look at all those irrational ideas that in those moments you have in your head; and try to look for the calm, until all those thoughts are placed and stop associating and your confused conscience begins to clear.

Then you will be using your mental power, when you begin to be aware of all those manifestations that arise within you, sometimes without any kind of explanation, that are inciting you to retreat, that are weakening you, while they rise unconsciously from the depths of your memory.

You can easily be captivated by everything that clusters in your mind. You can let yourself be guided by each of its signals that arise at every moment; through all that thoughtless movement of unconscious contents that often lead you to deception, without being able to move away from them.

It is transcendental for our psychic health that we make a cleaning, from time to time, of our mind, that we brighten our conscience, adulterated by so many false ideas that we invent to create alternatives to our own reality, when in this one we do not find any type of hope; when this one produces discouragement and inclines us to have a dark vision of life and of everything that happens to us.

We can incorporate, if we so desire, a new vision of the world, one that does not destroy us from within, that does not stagnate us, that improves us in every way. We can move away from that fantastic vision that our own imagination often proposes to us.

We only have to pay attention to everything we perceive, to our way of understanding it, to the kind of decisions we make at every moment, which then translate into actions that create a network of habits that envelop us with enough skill so that we do not realize it.

The best way is to be aware of all these processes that occur within us, and trying to use all the strategies and tools at our disposal to redirect in the best possible way much of the mental activity, which in normal conditions takes hold of us leading us to actions often unwanted; of which then, over time, we regret, because we unwittingly turn them into habits that make us lose a lot of our time, which is very valuable, and also our energy.

BE PRESENT

Being present is also a way to use your mental power, because it enables you to direct and stop your own thought that is represented in those moments in your mind.

When we wake up -when we are aware that this is happening-, we can become aware of the movement that is happening inside of us, that is indicating to us the way we have to think and that is taking over our own will.

When you are present you observe everything from stillness; there is a serene and authentic communication with your inner self. You are aware of many aspects that exist within you that normally go unnoticed, but that also influence in some way your own decisions.

When you are present you access who you are, you reconcile with yourself and your interest in knowing yourself, in examining yourself, in getting closer to who you have always been increases; it is as if all uncertainty disappears.

Time stops, and in those moments nothing interrupts that union with yourself in which you recognize yourself as you are.

When you are present you acquire a surprising knowledge about yourself, thanks to which you can establish a closer and more direct communication with that other world that is a little further on, with that lucid and clean space that is your consciousness without thought; that place away from mental noise and all the alterations that are usually reproduced and that end up producing a series of emotions that affect your state of mind.

When you manage to be present you are using your mental power; and when this happens, the observation that you make of each situation is different, because it no longer starts from a point of view that is governed by your mind, you simply limit yourself to observe, to look at reality in a natural way, without previous judgments that entangle you and push you to turn it into something very different from "what it really is".

When you are present, you perceive everything around you with different eyes. You become aware of every detail that is contained in the events that happen, and in this way you end up having a vision that adjusts to what each thing really is.

You attend to reality from "harmony", without entangling it with obscure beliefs that in a normal situation are usually represented in your mind, leading you to a vision far from the truth.

When you are present, your attention is not influenced by your judgments, nor is it altered by your reflections. You simply stand there, un-changing, maintaining balance without any res-ponse from you. You just remain neutral, without participating in whatever is happening; you just tolerate it without feeling the need to understand it in its totality.

You do not need to modify anything, because everything happens as it is supposed to happen at that moment. You don't have to think about anything, just pay attention to the way in which everything is settling down, in which everything is being resolved.

You can only be aware of the power of your mind when you are a "witness" of all that happens inside you, of that flow of thoughts with which you are constantly identifying yourself, creating a false self that is only an appearance and not "what you really are", in the depths of yourself.

UNCONSCIOUSNESS

If we do not stay awake we fall into lethargy: into a stupor that slowly eliminates us, while we remain subjected to our unconscious and unconcerned way of proceeding.

If we maintain this attitude over time, it will strengthen in such a way that it will increase until it extends to all our daily activities.

Our unconsciousness is therefore amplified in everything we do. It will make us live in a permanent disorder, leaving us hardly any space to be ourselves; it will make us move forward without us being able to stop, without us being able to stop and analyze the facts or any event that happens to us.

To live in the unconsciousness of the mind is to live in a dark sunset, where everything is reduced to what is established in each moment in your consciousness, without you being able to have any other desire, nor any other aspiration; it is as if you feel pushed to always maintain the same direction.

10. The power of understanding

When we use the full power of our mind, we attain comprehension of all things; we place ourselves beyond physical time, establishing a distance between our own thoughts and that which we are.

It is as if we place ourselves at the beginning and are able to understand everything: those experiences we have had and the many difficulties we have gone through that at the time we did not understand because our mind was reluctant to give us a reason, a convincing explanation.

All the teachings are within us, but we can only reach them if we are aware of the power of our mind; if we know how to observe beyond, directing our attention to what really matters, to what we really need in each moment of our life.

Therefore, we should all be interested in knowing how all those processes that exist within us work, which we often do not pay attention to because we do not consider them important. Rather, we live immersed in another reality constantly; in that reality that the mind proposes to us in a repeated way through the contents that arise from our memory and that catch our attention and make us stay for a long time focused on a series of topics that do not lead us anywhere, and that are not very useful either.

Everything has an explanation, we only have to try to understand all that succession of contents that rise in our mind, within a disorder allowed by ourselves.

We will only have to look at our own reasoning to realize how we are interpreting reality; that is where our understanding of the world comes from.

The key lies in the way we decipher the messages that come to us from outside; whether or not we stop to perceive all those beliefs that contaminate us and take over our judgments and our own reason.

We will soon understand that the situation in which we find ourselves comes from there, from the way we have of integrating our ideas; of ordering our thoughts; of using our reason.

We must understand our mind. In this way we will stop being asleep, we will not fall into self-deception, to which many times our way of thinking subjects us; by which we end up converting into absolute truths many things that are not true.

To find a way out of all the difficulties in which we are involved, we must first make sure we understand how our mind works; how our behaviors are accommodated to what we think at each moment; how we are somehow determined, limited by those contents that are accommodated in our consciousness until they come to dominate us.

We must come to understand how this machinery works, which on many occasions clouds our reason and which we often ignore.

Only if we understand how the activity of our mind is, we can know what its true potential is. We will come to understand that everything we do is embodied there, sometimes instantaneously.

This is the best way to come to an understanding of everything that happens to us, even everything we do unconsciously. It is the only way to stand up in a complete way against all those ideas that are determining us and that are forged in our mind, without us being very conscious of it.

In this way we will come to better understand our mental functioning; and we will know how to take advantage of all the power we have inside. It will be the best way to redirect our energy towards what is really worthwhile, towards what is more adaptive for us.

ADVANTAGES

It is that we reflect; then we will begin to see everything a little clearer. We will be more awake; we will come out of that darkness that sometimes spills inside ourselves, through a shadow of silent negativism, that little by little is gaining ground if we do not avoid it.

For us it can be a therapy: the understanding of all those resources that we have inside and that remain there, waiting for us to become aware of them.

If we go inside ourselves, we will find a whole extraordinary world. If we observe it, we will realize the enormous power that we all carry within us.

In this way, we will be able to transform ourselves, heal ourselves if necessary, controlling what is reproduced in our mind, changing all those contents when necessary.

We will find an explanation to all our contradictions. We will not remain paralyzed in inactivity. We will live associated with tranquility, traveling on our true path, following in the footsteps of our authentic purpose, far from the deception of the mind.

If we insist on this task of understanding ourselves more and more, we will have the opportunity to feel free from the bonds of our own thinking; free from the entanglements that our own mind sometimes tries to impose on us unconsciously.

Somehow, we will feel freer. We will eliminate all those mental movies to which we are accustomed, and the rest of the elements that we consider pernicious or that do not adjust to "what we really are".

We will understand everything that is reproduced in our consciousness: why some thoughts are joined with others, why we act under a disguise, and why the same images are repeated for a certain period of time.

We will discover our best talents; how our mental structure is articulated and where the origin of who we are lies.

All this will provide us with an understanding of our behaviors. We will get to the beginning, to the origin where "what we are" is based. We will go back to all those experiences that gave rise to our peculiar vision of the world, to our particular and subjective vision of reality.

If we look for the origin of everything that happens to us, we will also be using our mental power. It will be a very powerful tool for us, because to every adversity, to every misfortune, we will be able to find an explanation.

The light of our consciousness will shine, we will stop wandering aimlessly. We will evaluate all our anomalies in a more precise way; we will spend more time on the side of sanity; we will not allow ourselves to be obfuscated or subdued by all those difficulties and setbacks that some-times arise in life, closing all our possibilities of growth.

11. The power of resources

Sometimes we go through life with a series of limitations imposed by ourselves. We are incapable of seeing our talents; of using our best qualities that are already within us, but that we do not manage to glimpse because we do not really reach that level of consciousness that allows us to penetrate beyond to observe what we are: all that information that is there, in the deepest part of ourselves, that keeps a concordance with our "true being".

Only if we know ourselves can we use our best abilities, can we coordinate in the best possible way all that stored knowledge that is the fruit of past experiences.

To know and understand ourselves and to get out of the ignorance to which we are sometimes subjected, it is necessary that we discover all those resources that are within us, to be able to take advantage of them and benefit from them.

Sometimes they are exposed and at other times they remain hidden, until, thanks to our intelligence and a series of circumstances, we manage to locate them.

We must not allow a lack of knowledge of ourselves to lead us to live without observing our inner world. Our search for all that exists within us must be constant; it is the best way to perceive and appreciate our way of understanding reality, our way of reasoning and the way to take advantage of our best qualities, which in some cases remain hermetic in the depths of our "great inner universe".

The knowledge of what we are places us in a situation in which we can increase our own capacities and turn off everything that tries to dominate us, to subdue us, whether they are thoughts or unconscious impulses that take hold of us without any foundation.

HIDDEN POTENTIAL

When we are flooded with disillusionment and we feel sad and unhappy, and nothing favors us and we believe that everything is over, we can always count on ourselves.

It is possible to penetrate a little further and use our conscious look, to realize our strength, that we have a whole repertoire of hidden capacities inside that can propel us to produce intense changes in our life.

If we really intend it, we can benefit from all those qualities that we all carry inside, in that wide inner world where the transcendent is stored, that which can protect us from conflicts.

It is there that we find all that is extraordinary in us, that which makes us strong and leads us to enthusiasm.

Our best qualities are still there, within ourselves. Sometimes we discover them and bring out our best potential; at other times we do not pay as much attention to all that is good in us; and many aspects, which we can develop, remain stored there, without us taking advantage of them.

It lies beyond

The best in us lies beyond our thoughts, beyond what usually appears in our consciousness. It is hidden in that space where we can find ourselves, in that level of consciousness that is not contaminated by thoughts.

Only from there we can be reborn, be ourselves again, because only there we can realize "what we really are" and what we could become.

It is a space of creativity in which you get to feel really free to take the direction that best suits what you want to be, your true path.

You are not influenced by the deceptions of the mind or by all those false beliefs that you have been developing over time and that you have been making your own, but that actually have nothing to do with "what you are", since they are just a mere illusion: they are creations that you have been developing in your own mind over time, through all those interpretations you have made of reality.

When you look a little further, you find yourself, and that is where your true power lies; that is where you can discover your best qualities, your greatest potential.

You find no impediment, no obstacle that prevents you from developing all those qualities that you can discover about yourself and that are there, freed from the usual prejudices and impediments that you find in your mind.

All our qualities are still there, although we do not see them apparently and we do not use them because of that lack of knowledge, or because in many moments our attention was lost in other matters, pending other issues that often are not so important to us.

Sometimes we remain pending on a whole amalgam of contents that in the end, in reality, are not very useful for us either.

We tend to waste time, and much of our energy, focusing on mental elements, always thinking the same thoughts, without this task being really productive for us.

How to discover it

Only if we observe ourselves and pay attention to our inner world, we can discover our true possibilities and we can use them to our advantage.

If you look inside you will find all your potential, which is stored there; although it often goes unnoticed because we do not pay enough attention to those things that are really important to us.

You just have to establish contact with your inner world to realize all these peculiarities that you possess and that differentiate you from the rest; it is the only way to bring them to light and to develop them properly, and to be able to take advantage of all that are our gifts, which are related, ultimately, with the best of ourselves.

In a way, everything starts from observation, and from that moment where one is aware of the processes that are working internally; in such a way that we can intervene on them and make some necessary modifications, thus achieving to take advantage of all the potential that we carry inside, but that we do not take advantage of because we are not too aware of its existence.

Everything is, in fact, in the way you use your mind. That is where your most important potential comes from.

You can only discover it if you know yourself, if you know all those intricacies that exist inside you that are only visible if you observe them carefully, if you are curious to investigate what is beyond what you see, what is beyond your usual mental mechanism; the one that makes you repeat thoughts without further ado, over and over again, until you finally end up performing an action related to those thoughts.

Only if you know yourself can you take advantage of all your potential, all that potential that is hidden in a place that we do not usually access due to lack of habit, of habit; because before we prefer to be attentive to other kinds of stimuli, to other kinds of information that are easier to access.

12. The power of action

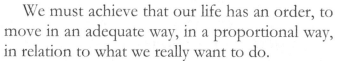

We must achieve that our life has an order, to move in an adequate way, in a proportional way, in relation to what we really want to do.

If we know how to take advantage of everything that favors us, our decisions will be more correct; we will be more coherent with ourselves, because everything will go in the same direction. There will be a greater precision in our actions, which will be adjusted to what we really think we should do at each moment.

From tranquility, and with good disposition on our part, we can observe the birth of all our behaviors. We only have to pay attention to all those thoughts that become visible in our conscience; that we feed every day, although they lead us to suffering and always draw us a landscape, inside us, discolored and lacking in meaning.

The basis on which everything we do is sustained is found in our thoughts; if in these there is no order, there is obfuscation and they are not understandable, they will be associated with similar behaviors; in them we will notice all that disorder that we sometimes contain within ourselves.

Everything that manifests itself outside, therefore, is first agitated inside, through a series of mental contents that accumulate until they finally transport us to a determined action.

This is how we function. When we want to introduce some change, we must pay attention to everything that is influencing us at the time of acting; observe the thoughts that most persist in our mind at that moment.

Thanks to our mental power, we can become aware of all these processes. In this way we can glimpse a clear explanation to everything we do, being aware that all that rests first in our own mind; it is where it is first assembled and built without us having the opportunity to observe it carefully.

Our mental power is based on this, on knowing how to control this system to reestablish the balance when necessary, so that our actions are the result of a conscious attitude, which is always in function of what we really want to do, deep within ourselves.

If we have the ability to appreciate it, we will have the opportunity not only to moderate it, but also to understand ourselves much better.

KINDS OF ACTIONS

There are two kinds of actions: one is what we do unconsciously and in most cases we are not very happy with it, because maybe it is not what we would like to do at that moment or it is different from what we understand should be our purpose; and on the other hand there are the actions we do in a conscious way, through the use of our will, which are related to what we really want to do, because we understand that this is the best way to achieve what we want or to reach our "true purpose".

When we do not act, we limit ourselves to wait for our mind to propose ideas, thoughts, in such a way that when certain contents are repeated frequently, they lead us to act in that direction, without us being very conscious of this and without us knowing how to put a brake on and control this process.

When we are not focused on what really matters, we do nothing to reveal ourselves, to conveniently manage our behaviors and change direction. We simply allow ourselves to be consumed by habits that operate on us in an arbitrary way, eliminating our will and originating in us a programming that accumulates and does not stop.

In the end we fall into bewilderment, we let ourselves be carried away by the seduction of what we should not do.

EVERYTHING IS RECORDED

Everything we do is engraved in our memory, so we must take care of our behaviors.

In reality, each one of our behaviors reinforces the programming that we have been manufacturing within ourselves. If we understand this well, we will understand that this whole repertoire of actions, which we repeat daily, is modeling us, making us "what we are".

Much of the information that spreads through our brain is the result of our contact with the outside world, of each and every one of the experiences we have in our environment.

We feed our mind with all that information that we gather from outside. Depending on the route and the path of our own actions, we create a mental re-recording of contents that we store in our memory.

Later, when we have to reflect on a subject, or reason about a specific topic, we will use the information from this inventory that we have stored and that we are cultivating day by day with new information.

FOCUSING ON A TASK

Our mind, in general, controls us without us being very conscious of it. It takes over us through a train of repetitive thoughts that flood our consciousness with a myriad of unconnected images that spring automatically from the depths of our memory.

The only way to cope with this whirlwind of forms is to centralize our attention on a specific focus. The most effective way to achieve this is to perform the task over a long period of time.

To do this we have to focus on what we have to do and be very careful not to abandon that activity, even if we do not have the desired reinforcement or reward at first.

We have to try to continue doing that task for a prolonged period of time, until it becomes a habit and with time it becomes less difficult.

Once we achieve it, we will do it mechanically; and while we are performing that task, our mental activity will only be focused on that subject and not on other kinds of matters.

It is a matter of focusing our mind on a certain action, and maintaining it for a certain period of time. Little by little a whole series of thoughts related to what we are doing at that moment will arise; the rest of the mental contents will fade away and stop influencing us. If we extend this action in time, our mind will only focus on what we are doing.

In reality, it is only when we act that we are able to extend our focus of attention. When we limit ourselves only to observing our own thoughts, there is no fixed or prolonged focus of attention, because the mental content varies very quickly and the images of which we are aware evaporate quickly giving way to the next ones.

When we perform an action, our mind is only focused on what we are executing at that instant. Many other thoughts are left aside and gradually disappear as we continue to concentrate on that particular task.

Therefore, if we want our mind to be focused only on a particular subject, the best way is to focus on a task and keep it over time.

In this way, most of our thoughts will be related to that subject, and the rest will gradually disappear as they find no use.

CONCENTRATION

When you decide to perform a specific task, with the effort not to deviate too much from that activity, you must keep in mind that there are times when you make a pause and stop performing that task.

In those moments you must be very focused to continue performing that action; those moments are the most delicate, when we stop performing a particular action because we do not find a reinforcement or a reward in what we are doing or a result is not visible or the expectations with which we have started that particular action are not met.

In these cases our tendency is to abandon that activity immediately and dedicate ourselves to something else. We are not aware that in those moments we may be invaded again by other different thoughts, which will almost certainly lead us to another type of action that surely deep down we do not want to perform, but that we feel obliged to do by the tendency of our thoughts, by the repetition of the same contents constantly in our mind.

This would be the reason why in many occasions we end up doing something that in reality we do not want; something that in reality is not what we had planned to do, in such a way that later we are not happy with ourselves when we see that we have done a series of things that we should not have done, when we become aware that we should have dedicated our time to other more productive matters for us; that all this has been caused by that lack of control that in most of the occasions we have over our own mind, over our thoughts, for abandoning that action that deep down we want to do but that many times we abandon it because we do not find in the short term an immediate reinforcement or satisfaction.

Sometimes many thoughts accumulate in all the immensity that is our mind. There are moments in which there is an enormous activity, depending on the hours of the day.

There are periods that are more conducive to creativity than others. If one knows oneself well, one can easily detect which ones they are and can select them to perform the tasks that require more effort and attention.

RESULTS

Maintaining an action for a long time entails a difficulty: if we do not see the reinforcement of a consequence, if during a period of time we do not obtain a reward, we do not achieve a result, it is easy to abandon that action and once again the same old thoughts come back to take hold of you, those that you would like to abandon from your mind once and for all; because they cause discomfort and in reality they are not very useful either.

Maintaining the same action, for a certain period of time, has the disadvantage of having an appropriate reinforcement, with a series of rewards and results that become visible so that we manage to maintain that activity constantly and we do not get diverted to other issues and influences that make us change our focus of attention.

It is important to be prepared when we face an activity that we want to do, to face those moments when we want to abandon it because we are not finding the expected results.

We have to be aware of the idea of keeping it as long as we are able, until it becomes a habit; then it will cost us less work to make the effort to prolong it, even if there is no short-term reward.

Only in this way our mind will focus on what we desire, because we feel that need or simply because we understand that this subject at that moment is very important for us.

13. The power of habits

The habitual functioning of the mind is based on a mechanism by which some contents arise repeatedly, trapping all our attention, until some of them manage to lead us to a concrete action; then we also remain trapped in that action, for a time, until we abandon it and decide to attend again to that course of thoughts that arise in the mind continuously.

Many of our problems come from following an itinerary that is already previously marked in our own mind and that sometimes leads us nowhere.

We simply rush to follow a mental programming that is already established, by force of repetition, even if it is not healthy or does not cause us satisfaction in the long term.

This way of directing ourselves gradually fragments us from the inside. On the one hand, we allow ourselves to be carried away by everything that our mind dictates to us; and on the other hand, we have the impression that what we think or do at a given moment does not represent us very much; it is not in line with the person we would like to be.

And the fact is that everything is caused by all that succession of thoughts that are constantly repeated and that are associated creating a mental structure that little by little is expanding forming a series of related habits that submerge us in a world that is not ours.

WE GET CARRIED AWAY

Only when we see the magnitude of the consequences, we become aware of a series of signs that warn us that our life is not on the desired path.

Then we realize that what we are doing in those moments is incompatible with what we should be doing so that our actions are in accordance with what we really intend, deep down inside ourselves.

We can stay like this for an unlimited time, without seeing the consequences, resisting change, stubbornly refusing to give up all those habits that take up most of our time and that we continue to perform unconsciously, totally unconcerned about the consequences they may have for us in the future.

This inability to realize what we are doing, is caused by the operation of our own mental mechanism, which often imposes a programming that we ourselves feed, which establishes a series of repetitive behaviors that control us while we remain unchanged, limiting us to follow them, even if they are not entirely healthy for us.

Somehow we let ourselves go, at the same time that a habit is installed in us that determines us, that separates us from what we would really like to do.

We usually get used to functioning in this way, letting ourselves be carried away by every thought that appears in our conscience. We do not manage to break this circle to which we are accustomed, letting ourselves be carried away by our habits that little by little increase until in the end we become unconscious machines that let ourselves be dominated by our own mental system, without looking for a solution to all this confusion that many times we notice inside us that deprives us of feeling free and that we do not find the way to stop.

WE FEEL TRAPPED

These mental mechanisms, in the form of habits, trap us in such a way that they block us on many occasions, rob us of all initiative and prevent us from working towards the realization of our dreams.

Many times we feel trapped in a series of mental loops from which we cannot get out, we are not able to find a way out that allows us to break those vicious circles that often form within our own mind, that limit us in such a way that they do not allow us to develop properly. They limit our own personal transformation and many things we could do to improve ourselves.

CONSEQUENCES

If we allow ourselves to be governed by our own mind, we will go in the direction it sets us. Somehow we will go with the flow, repeating over and over again the same behaviors. We will keep the same thought structure without stopping to observe the consequences of following certain ideas.

If we are satisfied with this mechanism, we will be inclined to mechanically execute all those habits that govern us, without understanding that we can modify them; transform our own behaviors into other very different ones that are more in line with what we really want to do.

If we manage to execute multiple habits that do not have as a purpose what we really want, we will find in ourselves a lack of integrity that will not favor us.

We will live in a stormy incoherence that will gradually drag us down; we will not feel balance; we will stubbornly continue to maintain an indefinite stream of actions that lead us nowhere.

When there is disorder within us, we fall into incoherence, we stop acting in a constant way and little by little our will disintegrates considerably, to the point that our mind takes over and becomes the guide of all our behaviors; in the background it annihilates everything that we would really like to do: that which is in line with our "true purpose".

If we leave our mind to its own free will, it is possible that we will be overcome by a myriad of repetitive thoughts that will undoubtedly end up taking over us, capturing all our attention and consuming all the energy we have at our disposal on a daily basis.

WHAT TO DO

Our habits, our customs, shape who we are. Much of what we are is due to what we do on a daily basis.

We should not waste our lives by spending time on things that lead us nowhere. In reality, our days can be summarized in a succession of behaviors that have a specific purpose. Depending on the direction of these behaviors, our life will develop in one way or another.

If there is no restraint on our part and we support this way of conducting ourselves, we will have to resign ourselves to follow the movements dictated by our own mind; we will not have the possibility of developing our best qualities, because they will remain hidden and we will only pay attention to those elements to which we are subjected.

If we manage to understand and realize how this mechanism works, we can transform it, if there is a greater involvement on our part.

It is only a matter of putting our mental power to work, to be able to change this internal mechanism, entering into that territory where some thoughts are joined with others and applying enough clarity to lean towards those contents that favor us more, that have a greater relationship with what we really are, with what we think we should do.

We would get rid of all those habits that limit us, preventing us from using our time for what really matters.

We have the inconvenience of having to face all those mental habits that we have been nurturing without being aware of the consequences they have for us in the performance of our small daily actions.

It all depends on the type of habits we have created, especially at the mental level. If we have accustomed our mind to work in a certain way and then we want to modify it, because we understand that its operation does not produce a benefit, it will not be easy for us to make that change, since behind a habit there is a complex structure of neural connections that have been created and strengthened as we have been repeating over and over again the same process, the same actions.

We must be aware that it is through continuous practice, and with a large dose of patience, how we can transform all those habits that are not favorable and that are harmful to us, since they prevent us from doing what we should really do.

It is only possible to achieve this through an act of will on our part, because breaking with the mental habit, which is based on the repetition of the same thoughts, involves an effort to become aware that this occurs and what we can do to reach that control that allows us to focus only on what we consider to be relevant.

All these ideas can be quite useful to eliminate all those habits that make us waste unrecoverable time in activities that actually have no use; from which we can hardly take advantage.

Be aware

We have to be aware that there are mental habits in us against which we have to fight, overcome them, if we want to reach a higher level, a more conscious way of life, through which we have a greater control of ourselves; and above all of our mental functioning, which most of the times makes us work in an automatic and unconscious way, as if we were a robot.

When we set out to develop a new task and we intend to maintain it over time, everything will depend on being aware that this happens, that we will encounter this difficulty; and on the other hand also on the degree of will that we put when it comes to be above our own mental habit, not to get carried away by the tendency of our own mind to function in a mechanical way, in which one thought after another occurs, sometimes without any connection between them.

With proper training and continued practice, great achievements can be made. In this sense we can achieve to be above many of our mental habits, which lead us to function in an unconscious way and without hardly having control of ourselves; in such a way that all this prevents us in many occasions to realize what we really intend, that which has to do with our "true purpose" and with what we really want to do.

14. The power of control

In reality, we are victims of what we think, of everything that moves and evolves in our consciousness. In the end, we end up walking in the direction determined by our own thinking.

Everything that manifests in our mind then becomes evident in our behavior, in our attitude, in our way of doing things.

If you let your mind work freely, without a certain control, what ends up happening is that an endless number of unconnected and repetitive thoughts about a series of frequent contents, about which you have shown a certain interest before, come to your consciousness.

We only let ourselves be carried away by their vivacity, by their flashes that little by little absorb us and reduce our knowledge to the same old affirmations, since it is always the same movement to which this restricted mechanism adheres, which little by little limits us and separates us from what we are.

Our imagination, at times, also feeds in this way: without any control, without a clear direction on our part. It follows the traces that automatically emerge from our memory, without even examining whether they are real or not.

This is, let's put it this way, the mental functioning we have. It is up to us whether we improve it or whether we do not introduce any modification.

In reality, our mind will function the way we allow it to function. If we do not exercise a certain control, it will always use the same gear, which will make us function practically always in the same way, through a programming that is created based on the repetition of a series of behaviors over time.

This is how the mechanism of our mental activity works; it is what determines us, in reality.

Our development depends on how we use it: if we get used to it and follow all its guidelines, we will live subject to it; if, on the other hand, we manage to eliminate, even at certain times, some of its automatic processes, we will make better use of our intelligence.

If we pay attention, our mental movement oscillates through thoughts that flow one after the other and dictate to us what we should do. In general, we allow ourselves to be led by this system.

If we have the ability to find the right information, we will know this mechanism, we will be able to use it in a more precise way.

We must be aware of everything that is hidden within us; of everything that excludes us from life, from our relationship with others; of everything that leads us to make mistakes; that makes us restless; that leads us to permanent worry; that little by little isolates us from the world, causing us to abandon ourselves to indifference.

It is necessary that we stop, at least for a moment, to restrain those ideas that are not in line with who we are; that which causes us an imbalance that in the end ends up dominating us, because it invades us completely.

We have to stop living chained to this incessant mental mechanism that creates wrong impressions of the world and of ourselves.

We must do everything possible to eliminate all that mental clatter - all those elements that move without direction - that lead us to move away from reality, to spend our energy on things that deep down do not cause us real satisfaction.

THE CONTROL OF THOUGHT

It is not always our mind that exercises a control over us, there is the possibility that we are the ones who impose an order, we estimate the most suitable thoughts to put our attention on them.

If we do it this way, we will be using our mental power. We will stop, in some way, that automatic mechanism, to which we are accustomed, that facilitates the repetition of one thought after another in a constant way.

Our thoughts can go in any direction we wish. We can choose the subject and, with a certain mastery, achieve a flow of content related to that subject for a prolonged period of time.

If necessary, we can take control when we want to; drive our ideas, propose the matters we should think about and direct the inclination of all those images that ascend to our consciousness and spread and expand impulsively.

We can direct everything that propagates through our mind, restricting what we deem unnecessary or that does not bring us any benefit.

Observation

It is also important that there is a connection with that space from which you can observe everything that happens to you internally; to be able to renew everything that is causing you harm, that is robbing you of stillness or condemning you to live a life without a clear purpose, without a firm objective.

When this happens, we get to observe, more deeply, all that exists within ourselves. We perceive all the representations, the images, that circulate through our consciousness, with the faculty to let them pass, without being affected by them and making us lose our balance at any moment.

To stop the mental noise, that endless train of one thought after another to which we are constantly subjected, the best way is to stop and observe ourselves, paying attention to what is happening in our own mind.

In this way, to the extent that we observe all that flow of mental contents, we begin to exercise a certain control over what is happening in our own mind.

When we observe it, we do not allow ourselves to be influenced, nor do we allow ourselves to be affected by every thought that springs from the depths of our memory into our consciousness.

In this way we can place ourselves at the margin of its content, thus achieving that it does not have an influence on us; it is the best way to separate ourselves from that mental noise and not let it influence us too much.

In these moments of deep observation, we gain control of our mind and therefore of ourselves, so that we can manage to lead our own thoughts and direct them in the way we want, leaving aside all those toxic contents that often assail us and prevent us from seeing our true path, that divert us from what we are, leading us along other paths that have nothing to do with what we feel we are, deep within ourselves.

It can become an effective way to reach a certain control of what happens in our mind; and therefore to a mastery of ourselves, of what we think and what we do repeatedly in our daily life; it can become a tool of the first order, in order to appease all those useless and toxic mental contents that often flood our consciousness for no reason.

Finding the origin

If we find the origin of that which gags us, we can penetrate further and observe its movements, see on what idea it is based; how we interpret reality at that moment.

Knowing what it is that destroys us, we can find out its trajectory, what kind of thoughts are associated with it that make us go to permanent disaster.

It is a quite practical way to control your own thoughts, to direct them, leading them along a specific path, at the same time that you eliminate those frequent contents that flood your mind and that, being too repetitive, consume your energy without actually leading you anywhere.

If we can do this, we will have a valuable tool to remove those thoughts that cause us emotional damage, that are toxic or that do not produce any benefit.

Knowing this is of utmost importance, as it is a way to eliminate all that mental activity that constantly overwhelms us with a myriad of different thoughts that are repeated endlessly for most of the time.

To discover your mental power is to know how to get to the beginning, to that moment where your impulses start and take hold of you; to that moment where your thoughts rise to the surface of your consciousness and stick a stamp on it, in such a way that it ends up calling your attention -even if it is unreal- and you end up following it.

Establishing order

Therefore, we must establish an order in this mechanism and not neglect it, otherwise we will act in an unconscious way, following only what those thoughts mark us; although in some cases it is not the best for us.

If we have enough information about it, we can stop it, examine the thoughts or let them pass. We can prevent the same thoughts from repeating themselves, so that there is an order and not an obsession to always be thinking about the same subjects.

We have to find the way to omit them, not to let ourselves be infected by the senselessness, by all that succession of forms that are associated in our consciousness and confuse us, blocking us, making us experience a reality very different from "the one that is".

THE CONTROL OF ATTENTION

We tend to move away from what is really important to us, because somehow we allow ourselves to be dragged by a myriad of influences, both external and internal.

In the end, our attention is diverted from what is really important and leads us to waste considerable time on other matters that are not so relevant to our psychological well-being, or to the achievement of those goals we have previously set for ourselves.

When we see ourselves disoriented and something disturbs us inside, we must change that which oppresses us, which leads us to confusion. We must move away from where we are focused at that moment; it is the only way to lower the intensity of everything that is being defined in our consciousness, in those moments that are being represented in our mind.

It is the best way to contribute so that all those thoughts that are being diffused do not become generalized, so that they do not increase and do not enlarge to the point that they become concentrated in a structure that later will be almost impossible to eliminate.

Thoughts are going to repeat themselves over and over again if your mind is not focused on a particular focus of attention. If you let your thoughts flow without any control, it is like leaving an open door to an endless number of contents that come from your memory and that will not stop flowing until you do not fix your attention on a certain point.

Depending on the circumstances in which we find ourselves in each period of our life, if we know how to use the right strategies and we manage to focus on what really matters, on what is relevant to us, we can achieve all the goals we set for ourselves, We will stop wasting time in other irrelevant matters that little by little are wearing us out unnecessarily and making us lose much of our energy, while we keep our attention fixed on mental contents that do not really solve our doubts or help us to solve the difficulties that we encounter daily in our daily work.

Focusing on a specific point

It is normal that our mind wanders from one thought to another, so that many times these thoughts are not related.

To avoid this, it is necessary to focus our mind on a specific point and remain centered on that subject, trying not to deviate too much; in this way everything we think will be related to that specific aspect.

This can be done in two ways: through action -while we act we usually keep our attention fixed on what we are doing-; and through meditation, through the internal observation that we can make of our own thoughts.

In this way we can also make the effort to focus on a very specific type of content, trying to avoid straying towards other types of thoughts that we want to mitigate, that we want to put aside momentarily, because they tend to occupy a space within our own consciousness, forcing us to focus our attention solely and exclusively on them, so that they lead us into an endless loop in which we are constantly repeating the same content, the same images and ideas in a mechanical way.

Once you put your focus on that content, it is advisable, for this method to work, to perform a series of activities related to that topic, trying to maintain -this is very important for this strategy to work- as much as possible that task over time; so you must be very attentive to those moments when you lose concentration or you feel like disconnecting.

In those cases you should try, by all means, to maintain that activity or that task, even if in those moments you do not find the necessary reinforcements or the expected results.

You must try to continue executing the same action firmly, so as not to give place or not to create that pause, that space in your consciousness so that other kinds of different thoughts can occupy it, so that they can distract you and lead you towards other kinds of actions; in short, towards another unwanted focus of attention.

This requires you to be patient, being aware that at the beginning it will be more difficult to obtain visible results, but with a little effort and practice you will manage to form the right habit to get, whenever you consider it necessary, to put your focus of attention on what really matters, on what makes you see clearly your main purpose, your "true purpose": what really satisfies you and what you understand that is beneficial and useful for you.

This can be a great strategy if you put it into practice, if you repeat it over time. In the same way it is also advisable that you alternate it with moments in which you can do some meditation exercises, practice conscious observation. All this will lead you to achieve a mastery over your own mind that will make you know and experience that great force within you that is your "mental power".

Difficulty

Sometimes we find it difficult to focus our mind on a certain point, and thus abandon all those thoughts that distract us, that are useless because they do not lead us anywhere.

When we want to break with this process and establish a new focus of attention, we find the difficulty that our mind is not accustomed to this process, to this new focus, so it will be difficult to overcome our own mental habits.

It is difficult to concentrate our attention on a single point; we allow ourselves to be distracted by thousands of stimuli around us and also within ourselves.

Not everyone succeeds, as we often find it difficult to maintain our concentration for long enough on a given subject.

Mental power

He who truly uses his mental power is the one who is able to focus on what really matters and does not let himself be carried away by other influences that may hinder his attention at that moment; and he does so because he is aware that this happens previously, because he has observed how this mechanism works and has realized what can distract him, and when the time comes he is able to stop any stimulus that tries to divert him from what he is paying attention to.

The one who really gets to use the power of his mind manages to attend only to the contents that interest him at a given moment; he is able to focus on them and stay that way for a while, without any other influence being able to take him away from them.

In this way he can use his mental power to inquire further into a given subject, without being affected by external influences. In this way he can attain a certain degree of knowledge of whatever he is interested in.

What we achieve

If we accustom our mind to fixate on the same focus of attention, it will forget the rest of thoughts and will not attend to other kinds of mental contents that may arise from our memory. It will only attend to those images and thoughts that are related to that specific focus.

So, if in some period of your life you are invaded by a series of harmful thoughts, and you are trapped in a mental loop from which you cannot get out, the best way to solve that situation is to focus your mind towards a subject that is to your liking, that is of your interest, that you understand that it does not produce any emotional damage, that it is good for you.

If we use the strategy of focusing our mind towards a concrete subject, we will achieve that other kinds of thoughts do not take hold of us. While we remain focused on a specific task, we get that our mental processes are directed towards that topic and not to others, so that the completion of a set task causes them to disappear from our mind many contents that often occupy our consciousness and that are not too useful, since it is a material that is repeated frequently managing to occupy most of our mental space, which makes us have our eyes on a number of issues that are not really so important to us.

All this leads us to be attentive to all these elements and at the same time we divert our attention, we do not keep focused on what really matters; on what should be our main task, which is that activity that should be related to our "true purpose", to our main function.

Only when we focus on a certain point, and we manage to direct all our attention and thoughts towards that specific place, is when we reach a certain mastery of all that mental process that occurs within ourselves.

CONTROL OF IMPULSES

Sometimes, we are indifferent about those things that are really the most important, out of ignorance or ignorance of the consequences; although later we regret having done it.

Somehow we justify ourselves for our way of acting compulsively, without reflecting or observing what really matters.

And it is that, many times, we act accelerated, as if isolated from what we really are, and we go through life without paying attention, without extending ourselves too much, disregarding the details of everything that happens inside. We go astray, without knowing how to distinguish what is bad or good for us.

We function by impulses

Many times we function by impulses that we ourselves are favoring, giving way to them without prejudice to the consequences that these can bring us.

These impulses that arise with such force, spread very quickly without us being able to do anything to avoid them.

We simply abandon ourselves to them, we allow them to spread within us without doing anything to diminish their intensity, to eliminate them in any way.

They alter our inner world, because sometimes they are very persistent. They occupy all our internal space in such a way that in the end they incline us to carry out certain behaviors, if we do not know how to stop them.

They are distributed without hardly giving us time to understand them, to understand their sense; to carry out a reflexive reasoning on their meaning and their purpose.

We hardly have time to explore them in depth, to approve or reject them. We also do not know their origin; although if we analyze them a little we realize that they are executed in an unconscious way, since they arise in an automatic way and rise above us and overflow us and repeat themselves until they lead us to a determined action.

Our impulses, in a way, subdue us. They are like an energy that arises suddenly and silently spreads within us until it envelops us and forces us to perform a series of actions that, if they are very repetitive, we maintain over time.

Impulses are sometimes very powerful, because their impetus can erase our calm and can lead us to change our objectives, to incline us to vary our course, and sometimes create an instability that can lead us to disorder, especially when we do not exercise a certain control over them; when we let ourselves go and allow them to dominate us when they emerge from the deepest part of ourselves.

They have enough ability to make us lose control, to take us where we don't want to go; which makes us lose our balance many times, when we see that we have sacrificed our valuable time on things that are not really worth it.

Instead of placating them, sometimes, in an incomprehensible way, we let ourselves be guided by them, until we recognize that we have been wrong, that it has been a mistake on our part to act that way.

If we allow ourselves to be flooded by everything that permeates our mind and we give way to all that flow of impulses that arise in chain, that take hold of us, we will slide through life as mechanical beings, being the living expression of our unconscious programming, of our most elementary impulses, that little by little separate us from what we really are, from what we should do at every moment.

Control

Our mental power also consists, in some way, in knowing how to manage and control all these impulses that many times take hold of us -of our own will- and lead us diligently towards another direction that in the end does not satisfy us.

If we get used to exercise some control over them, we will see that with time they will begin to act in a more and more dispersed way, that little by little they will affect us less.

If we learn to correct them, every time they are exposed, we will see how they move away from our attention; how, little by little, they stop being so impetuous, so hasty.

Only from deep meditation, from slow reflection, we can take control of these impulses; because only from that situation that allows us to go deep inside ourselves, we can notice them, see their influence and in this way we manage to isolate them, to the extent that we observe them.

In this way we recover the control of ourselves, by diminishing this energy that emerges in an unconscious way and that little by little is increasing until it makes us act in a certain direction.

If we are conscious of them we can correct them, regulate them, avoid them in some way. We can make sure that they do not dominate us, even if they are very insistent.

In this way they will not affect us and they will fade little by little, as we postpone them, directing them, preventing them from renewing themselves and resurfacing again.

When they stop manifesting, we will see an improvement, a transformation in which we will find a clarity that will cover us with a brightness that will make us be reborn.

BENEFITS

You can create a new world, but always from the consciousness, controlling at all times the content and objects that arise in that dimension, in that space that is away from the automatic thoughts of the mind.

Thanks to this you can take control of what happens inside you, which will influence your behavior, your actions: they will be much less mechanical, automatic.

You will walk through life in a more conscious way, knowing at all times what you are doing, the reason why you are doing it; as well as the consequences that this particular action will have in the future.

We can experience the power of our mind when we are the ones who direct it; when we control in a way its functioning, its movements, many times unequal, that lead us to have contrary thoughts, in many occasions, in a short space of time.

If we take control, we will come out of the darkness, we will not allow ourselves to be trapped by our own thoughts; we will manage to reach calm, correct our mistakes, observe in the depths of ourselves all that we are; away from any influence, from any stimulus that wants to plunge us into deception, away from our "true essence".

Then we will be able to emerge, to overcome ourselves, to surpass all those mental walls that we sometimes create for ourselves through limiting thoughts.

We will find clarity, observing our mind freed from the influence of imagination and any other obstacle that determines it.

In those cases you will see that all the difficulties disappear -which is usually where they go - and suddenly there will be nothing to push you in those moments to perform a particular action.

All the inconveniences disappear, you see yourself capable of doing anything, but at the same time you feel distanced from all those stimuli that try to divert you from that place where you begin to find a coherence that did not exist before.

From that moment on you begin to realize that you can moderate what happens there.

As a reward we will reach tranquility, if we manage to take control of all these processes that arise within us and that are slowly absorbing us. We will find "clarity" in those matters that we are unable to understand; we will act in a more independent way and we will improve communication with ourselves, within that space away from the noise of our own thoughts.

15. The power of transformation

Sometimes anguish invades us and we lose our balance, we feel an inner torture, many times without knowing its nature. If we attend to that which afflicts and consumes us, we will investigate the causes, we will go to the bottom of the problem.

This inconsistency has its origin in your own mind; that never stops fabricating evocations that can destroy you or recover you, depending on the contents that manifest themselves and then become entrenched with the passage of time.

At other times a division is also created in you, a fracture, between what you think and what you end up doing; this is what produces that there is no permanence in your behaviors, in your way of thinking.

It is always necessary that we find balance, when confusion reigns within ourselves; that we separate ourselves from everything that disturbs us, that is depressing or disconcerting us; that is leading us to an abyss with no way out.

Thanks to the power of our mind we have the capacity to repair what is destroyed; to resolve our doubts and to be guided again by logic and reason.

We can transform ourselves if we know how to find the explanations, through a deep reflection on everything that limits us, that condemns us to live a life prostrated in discouragement, that little by little is precipitating us to an unhappiness that is spreading throughout our body, that is diverting us from ourselves and limiting our own growth.

It is the only way to resolve our internal conflicts, to control all that mental activity full of inconsistencies that makes us live in a permanent discord with ourselves; that makes us spend all the energy we have in useless fantasies that little by little are installed within us and separate us from the real world, from that which we perceive outside, in our immediate environment.

Then we will be able to get rid of what is destroying us inside, if we have enough strength to deviate from all that is determining us.

If we free ourselves from that which disturbs us, that which clutters us, we will find a stillness that will help us to orient ourselves in the midst of all those difficulties and inconveniences that we encounter in life.

SUFFERING

Our suffering, in reality, has its origin in all those thoughts that intertwine, almost in a mechanical way, that are related to a way of reasoning that increases only the negative aspects, that contemplates a way of understanding life only from misfortune and misfortune.

All this creates a mental structure in us that we can undo, but only if we have the necessary temperance.

It is maintained in the time

There are problems that remain in us for long years, often because we have reached the habit or the habit of living with them. We do not feel the need to eliminate them, to begin to produce changes to diminish the possible influence that they can be having on our own well-being.

In the meantime, these problems spread until they take us to a limit that breaks our internal balance and our life becomes a disorder that slowly drowns us.

That which causes us suffering can remain within us for a long time, we can increase it without realizing it. Sometimes we do not feel the urgency or the need to change; we put it off until later.

We continue walking, but that restlessness remains within us, it stays there, caged, and continues affecting us and creating an internal discomfort to which we do not dedicate time because we have our focus of attention elsewhere.

And the fact is that, on many occasions, we make life difficult for ourselves. We are aware that there is an imbalance inside, but we are not ready to initiate the appropriate changes to get out of that difficulty that we are getting stuck inside, intoxicating our inner peace.

We have to rise up, when necessary, to straighten the course, to suppress all those elements that remain hidden and that lead us to confusion, that distract us and that do not provide us with "clarity" so that we can have an objective vision of things, of the reality that surrounds us and of ourselves.

If we allow all these representations to develop, they will remain in time and will gradually increase, until we get used to them. Therefore, it is essential that we act in time, that we are not indifferent, when it comes to suppressing all those manifestations that spread in our mind with the idea of confusing us.

We must stop obeying everything that our mind proposes to us, because this often does not conform to what we really need or want deep inside ourselves; in such a way that it ends up distancing us from our own happiness and leads us to suffering, which is caused by this way of thinking and acting quite far from what we are, or what we want to be.

The mind can be both light and darkness; it depends on the use we make of it. It is possible that we make disappear for a time everything that arises in it; or we can follow unconsciously only those contents that cause us suffering and stay that way for a certain time.

We can be slaves of our own thoughts, so we will not be able to use all the potential that is hidden within us.

The one who uses the power of his mind is the one who knows how to transcend all that suffering produced by his own thoughts; the one who knows how to guide himself and walk the path of his "true purpose", where his "true nature" is, where everything originates, in that space of your inner world where you really feel free and which can only be accessed through a proper conscious observation, through the correct use of your own mind.

Using your full mental potential depends on you. Not everyone makes a correct use of the mind, many get carried away by everything that happens in it, reaching a suffering that never stops, that always continues in them.

To be conscious

We can promote new changes in us if we use that hidden power that we all carry within us to control, in some way, all that which reproduces and multiplies in our consciousness; all those stimuli that come from the deepest part of ourselves and that affect us and determine what we are.

The main condition to get rid of this somber vision of life is to be aware of it, when it takes root in our own consciousness. Then, we must understand that it is only an invention of our mind, which we maintain for a while because we lose "clarity" and we only observe that which shadows our vision of things.

If we realize this in time, we will have the facility to abandon all those thoughts that sometimes wave through our mind with the idea of taking over us.

If we are sufficiently disposed, we can stop following the current of everything that immobilizes us, that prevents us from developing our best qualities and that makes us live in a permanent restlessness, in a place where only suffering and internal division reside.

When the world is paralyzed, you must keep walking, focus on everything that favors you; return to stillness and put aside your inner conflicts.

It becomes necessary for us to realize the path we often tend to take, which is often a path of suffering, where we find no hope.

We simply move towards it because we experience a tendency to follow certain beliefs and ideas driven by our own mental focus.

To know your mental power is to be aware that you can modify the functioning of your own mind; that you can discover how it works: what its activity is like, what it is that causes us to settle in suffering and stay there for so long.

Resolving the past

If you know how to use the power of your mind, you will be able to wake up from that deep sleep in which you usually find yourself, where there is usually suffering that you create without knowing it, through the past.

You will be able to analyze your thoughts, by means of the conscious observation that you will be able to make on yourself; then you will be able to modify some interpretations that in your day you made of all those things that happened to you.

In a way, your mental power is in contemplating the past as it was, far from the unconscious interpretations that you made at the time, moving away from the truth.

Thanks to your mental power you can change everything that once confused you. You can resolve conflicts and stop your mind from floating in that constant noise of absurd thoughts.

FRUSTRATION

We are used to experiencing frustration every time we do not receive a reward for what we do. At those times we may not quite understand why we don't get a result.

We can let this feeling take hold of us and drag on for a while; or we can dig a little deeper to find out why there is a mismatch between what we thought up in our minds and the final result.

Many times we are passionate about an idea, but we do not stop to examine, calmly, if it can lead us to an uncertain situation or not; we do not have that habit.

We think that everything we intend will be fulfilled, without stopping to analyze all the details and circumstances that surround us; the difficulties we will encounter along the way and the strength we must have at certain times, when our will diminishes and we begin to lose interest due to the lack of results.

In these cases we must go to the birth of that idea, of that objective, to distinguish the reasons that have led us to embark on that purpose.

Once we know its origin, we will understand if it is reasonable, if it has a raison d'être and a foundation.

We will understand the limitations; if we will find the way clear, free; if the situation is favorable or we will end up finding distortions that we will have to solve if we want to reach a good port.

Our mental power helps us to understand all the difficulties we are going through, and in the same way it can also show us, if we know how to look for them, the solutions to each and every one of our problems.

It depends on how we interpret the information that we obtain from our own experiences. Everything we experience has its usefulness, even that which at the time did not turn out as we expected.

Our reward will be to be above frustration, above any difficulty, above that which paralyzes us, which prevents us from walking through life without any kind of suffering.

OVERCOMING DIFFICULTIES

Our life is built by overcoming obstacles; there are innumerable difficulties that we have to face throughout our life.

There are those who immediately look for a way out of all their problems; others do not focus so much on solving them, and let them join one with another until in the end it becomes difficult to find a way out of so much confusion.

And there are those who are used to live in difficulty; they always remain there, burned by their problems, without the slightest intention of looking for a way out.

They try to manage to survive in some way, but without devoting themselves entirely to make a radical change in their situation.

They are people who tend to postpone for the next day everything they should do to have a more abundant life. They remain immobile, paralyzed by each and every one of the inconveniences that life puts in their way at every step.

Sometimes, when they examine themselves, they feel that they should change some things, because they understand that they have a limited life - full of obstacles everywhere - that they are consuming in a hasty way without any enthusiasm and without any foundation.

They are content to resist, allowing themselves to be subjected to a repetitive life, without any benefit. They have no other pretension than to live a sad life; they do not feel a need to experience extraordinary experiences; to make changes; to point in another direction....

They recognize that their life is a constant torment, a permanent conflict to which they have become accustomed, without giving themselves the opportunity to achieve a little satisfaction.

Then they find discouragement -when that happens, it is difficult for them to get rid of it-; they begin to feel boredom, which slowly irrigates all over their body.

Mental power

If you know how to use the true power of your mind, you will know how to act appropriately, how to manage through life overcoming your own limitations; how to look for alternatives and modify what is necessary to overcome all those difficulties that arise daily.

If you know how to look inside yourself, you will discover how to overcome the obstacles that life presents you; you will be able to find possible solutions for each of the difficulties that appear.

Your mind is capable of overcoming the different problems that may arise, we only need to observe ourselves and then we will find the "wisdom"; this will help us to focus on what really matters, on what enables us to follow the path that leads us to our "true purpose".

He who knows how to use his mental power does not sink, does not let himself be destroyed by this frequent mental mechanism that leads us to anomaly, to disorder, because it ends up immobilizing us, stagnating us in a restlessness that leads us to anxiety, to live in a permanent contradiction, anchored in the past and in a thought without will, where we are not the ones who select the contents and the images that appear in our own consciousness.

He who uses his mental power, is above the setbacks: he does not let himself be carried away, in any way, by all that stream of thoughts, even if they occupy the center of his attention and are repeated with insistence.

When we live in permanent irritation and joy disappears from us, we must look at ourselves, use our mental power, and separate ourselves from all that which at that moment dominates us.

In that situation we have to start to reason, to get out somehow of that confusion that many times we suffer and that little by little is hurting us, afflicting us, until it starts to flatten us.

What we achieve

You can contribute to have a better life, if you forget all those obstacles that often take over your mind.

You can solve each and every one of the difficulties that life poses you, if you unload all that accumulated tension, the result of the pressure caused by many toxic thoughts that the only thing they do is distract you, by extolling some unconscious contents that are kept stored and that do not serve, that do not show you the right path: that which we must go through so that in your life there is an order, a certain direction that makes you always go upwards and that you do not stagnate among all that multitude of stimuli that confuse you and lead you to error, permanently.

We can discover everything that is good within ourselves; everything that tries to protect us from suffering and frustration.

All that remains within ourselves, and we can only conquer it if we know how to observe at a somewhat deeper level than usual; if we move away from the influence of the mind and leave its surface and go into that vast and wide inner space where we meet ourselves and end the domination of our own thoughts, which spring from our consciousness sometimes for no reason at all, so that we try to keep our attention on a certain subject.

If we know ourselves, we can use our mental power to be able to overcome the obstacles that come one after another in each of our past experiences.

It is the only way for us to stop being limited by that system of thoughts that often spreads inside and grabs us and does not make us enjoy life; that dominates us without us being able to abandon it; that twists and deforms reality and incites us to change course through a series of behaviors that make us lose our balance and self-confidence.

We will be able to realize how everything can be woven with obstacles, which in the end become an ascending wall that paralyzes and consumes us and erases our calm and creates a division within us that little by little fragments us, transporting us along a path that is not our own.

OBSERVE

When you face difficulties, you must understand and interpret correctly what is happening, to implement, in a precise way, the changes that are necessary to change those situations that are creating discomfort.

To do this you must focus all your attention on observing your internal dialogue and all those reasonings that are shown when you face something that is a problem for you and you do not find a way to solve it.

In this way you will connect with the "origin", where your confusion really starts. You will immediately discover all those representations that are creating a conflict in you that is messing up your reason, in such a way that they prevent you from finding a way out, finding a position that allows you to solve that situation that is stuck; it is the best way to orient yourself when something makes you uncomfortable and you do not understand the reasons why that complication exists.

However, there may be confusions in you of a great magnitude that require, on your part, a greater effort to restore your inner balance. In these cases you should be even more aware of the importance of making an effort to contemplate in a more reflective way how to deal with the difficulty.

Whenever possible we have to look inside ourselves to observe the reasons that often make us lose our calm, that emerge and drive us to create wrong reasoning about the world and ourselves, which gradually evade us from the existing reality and all those difficulties that arise in the day to day and to which we have to give them a solution, because otherwise they expand over time.

We have to learn to recognize the signs: everything that fills us with insecurity, that makes us unhappy and that is contaminating us inside. It is about becoming aware of everything that diverts us from reality; that drives us, without realizing it, to senseless suffering.

GO TO THE ORIGIN

You can transform your alteration into harmony; go to the origin where it all begins. It is about diving deep inside yourself, immersing yourself in your inner world, and looking for all those affirmations that occupy your mind, that determine you in such a way that all your thoughts are related to them.

It is about searching in the messages that we give ourselves, in all those mental contents that we constantly feed, unconsciously.

We can realize when they are born; how we fabricate them by putting all our attention on them. We will perceive that some are incomprehensible and that others only happen in our own imagination.

We will come to realize that many of our judgments are nothing more than interpretations of reality, that our internal discourse sometimes seems confused and that it does not have an order that allows us to group our ideas correctly.

We will understand that everything is based on what passes through our mind; that our consciousness is the place where everything originates, because that is where everything is represented, before leading us to a particular action.

The important thing is to know how to detect all this, to make a good diagnosis of the situation, to know in detail what we must change; and then we must also have a suitable method to achieve these changes and thus reach our own "personal transformation".

In this sense, we should always be attentive to everything that can interfere in our own personal development, in what prevents us from doing what we would like to do but we do not end up deciding because we always find thousands of impediments and inconveniences that slow us down, sometimes even leading us to the blockade; so that we see how little by little our own initiative, our will and even our own energy is being extinguished in many occasions.

Everything that prevents us from doing all that we should do, is within ourselves, part of our own mind and manifests itself in all those thoughts that arise again and again.

So that we end up identifying ourselves with them, to such an extent that we end up believing in everything we think. We take as truth many contents, just for the simple fact that they arise in our mind, which are transformed into what we end up thinking.

Our own transformation arises when we get to the "origin", when we discover the origin of all those absurd elements that go around in our head, which lead us to live in a permanent contradiction.

The important thing is to place ourselves at the beginning, where the mechanism begins to work; in this way we can control it in some way. If we know the procedure, the process, we can foresee what the next step is, what happens next, and in this way we can anticipate before everything is unleashed and no longer has a solution.

CHOOSING THE TYPE OF THOUGHTS

We must leave aside the useless thoughts, which remain for a long time in our conscience and which lead us to confusion and contrariness and which certainly do not serve to solve the daily difficulties that we frequently encounter. We must clarify as much as possible our mind, casting aside everything that holds us back, that fills us with obstacles.

We should only pay attention to what is useful to us, only to those contents in which we find "clarity".

You can give way to all that you consider favorable for you and eliminate what somehow breaks your balance: that which does not make you continue, progress, develop.

If you know how to stop, you can choose in advance the type of thoughts that are most favorable to you and ignore those that are not appropriate: those that you consider inopportune because they create obstacles that impede your growth.

ELIMINATE THE NEGATIVE

If we do not face everything that is deteriorating us, if we do not take care of ourselves and make the appropriate decisions, we will let ourselves be dominated by unhappiness, which will spread throughout our being, dissolving us, confusing us, orienting our life continuously towards a suffering that will cover everything with an irrational veil.

We cannot be indifferent to problems. We must grasp the causes, go to the base of all those sufferings that in many periods predominate in us and that in some way are determining us, because they are making us insecure; that we are losing our resistance.

We have to know how to properly manage that which destroys us, to stop cultivating it, to relegate it to the background. We cannot exalt the negative in us, we have to get rid of everything that creates confusion, that clouds our vision of reality, that irritates us or that entangles us, through a series of manifestations that cross our consciousness and cling to that space, repeating themselves over and over again.

We must not allow pessimism to take possession of us, to seduce us by taking over our thoughts.

Our motivation is a consequence of where we place our interest, internally. If we separate ourselves from our true objectives, insecurity begins to take hold of us, and in the end we allow ourselves to be covered by a mantle of vehement pessimism that limits us until it manages to separate us from everything that excites us.

We have to abbreviate the negative; if we elevate it, it will make us stumble again and again, it will envelop us and freeze our will and our desire to break through.

It is necessary that we use our mental power to put light where there is only darkness, to diminish everything that takes possession of us, that produces sadness or paralyzes us, that prevents us from having enough confidence to not hide behind a disguise, so that we do not run away from ourselves fleeing to nowhere.

Your mental power is based on knowing how to dominate many phenomena that occur within your inner world. This is possible if you have a good disposition, which you can develop through practice; in this way you can anticipate many mental processes that force you to put your focus of attention on a series of thoughts that frequently stand out in your consciousness.

It is just a matter of having the ability to stop all those impulses that somehow are altering you inside, occupying your mind, without having a solid base.

WE CAN BE REBORN

Thanks to our mental power, we can be reborn, resurface, return to ourselves when we feel separated from who we are.

We can find new arguments to transform ourselves, to modify what is necessary, to find again the strength to never leave our path, that path that is the true path we must walk to reach our "true purpose"; even if we have to transform ourselves again and again if necessary.

In some way we can reestablish, correct all those memories that have to do with difficulties, with obstacles. We can rebuild ourselves inside, improve our vision of things, restore that which is damaged.

You have the possibility to heal yourself, in case you need it, to come back to life if you only find dissatisfaction in yourself. You can stop being chained to the deception of your own mind and look beyond all those manifestations that have to do with "what you are", with your essence, from which you should never distance yourself.

PSYCHIC WELL-BEING

We can use our mental power to find a greater psychic well-being, to prevent all those thoughts that oppress us from gathering in our mind, that detach us from reality and lull us away, hiding our true potential; which if we have the opportunity to discover it is amazing, important, and is hidden inside ourselves.

In reality, we all depend on a process. We can live subordinated to it; or we can stop its mechanism and prevent many of these elements from becoming obstacles that prevent us from acting and developing conveniently.

The key lies in our way of proceeding. We can live in a permanent storm; or we can make our life light, pleasant, guided by reason and not be dominated by imprudence and by all those impulses that arise unconsciously from deep within ourselves.

Our psychic well-being depends on how we feed our beliefs; on our own vision of reality. If it is confused, our journey will be hesitant, we will allow ourselves to be dominated by all the tempest of difficulties that frequently befall us.

Our mental well-being is based, in this sense, on our way of interpreting the world; on our way of facing uncertainty; of wandering over frustration; of fighting against the inconveniences that often surround us relentlessly.

Everything is based on the way we understand disaster or prosperity; on how we convert our past experiences into knowledge, which will later make us proceed in a certain way.

Everything is closely related to the type of information that is reproduced in our mind. It depends on the concepts we use to qualify our experiences, what happens to us, how we consider the facts we observe, the type of conclusions we draw.

Knowledge

We have to reach our psychic well-being, otherwise we will continue to live in a daze, submerged in the disorders that are created in our own mind by a lack of knowledge, on our part, of these mechanisms that take place within ourselves.

If we acquire this knowledge, we will arrive at true understanding, which will settle in our consciousness and help us to establish an objective examination of reality whenever we need it.

In this way we will move away from our own contradictions and internal conflicts that we are often reinforcing without realizing it.

If we really intend it, we can move away from confusion, pushing away all those thoughts that cross our consciousness trying to obscure our vision of the world.

In reality, it is a matter of governing ourselves, solving all those internal complications that often disturb us, affecting our judgments and our way of understanding everything that happens to us.

This requires a great knowledge of our internal reality, of this mechanism and of these processes. Therefore, it is always advisable to seek within ourselves the necessary information to be able to control these movements that often lead us to confusion and to a wrong vision of reality and of everything that happens to us.

New mental order

Our strength lies in the good use of our mental power. We can manage to be above despondency if we manage to have control over all those manifestations that arise in our mind and that try to dominate us through repetitive and unconscious movements.

If we manage to manage all this, we can establish a new mental order that can free us from all those toxic contents that often settle in our consciousness and influence our way of interpreting the world.

If we are not aware that this is happening, they can increase and can incline us in a direction that does not suit us. That is why it is necessary for us to organize these elements that arise in our mind and that are included in our judgments and habitual reflections.

Psychic well-being appears when there is an order, a direction that does not go backwards. When there is a "harmony" that restores us, that strengthens us, making us see everything from serenity; which gives us time to rectify all those actions that are not profitable for us.

Our mental power is based on this, in being able to order and create new structures of thought that help us to see the "clarity" and to get out of that dark vision that we often have of ourselves, which slowly separates us from the world around us.

ABOUT THE AUTHOR

Manuel Triguero has a degree in Psychology from the Pontifical University of Salamanca (Spain). He has provided personalized help, as a counselor, to a large number of people.

In his books he transmits his own reflections on a series of topics related to self-knowledge and personal development. They are based on ideas and reasoning drawn from observation and his own introspection.

The purpose of his works is to reveal and make known the power that we all carry within us. To access it we first have to know ourselves. It is the first step to reach the "true personal transformation", to resolve inner conflicts and thus improve our lives in all those aspects that we can.

Made in the USA
Coppell, TX
03 May 2023

16362418R00132